SPIRITUAL GOLD

Reincarnation, Jesus, and the Secrets of Time

by

Paulinne Delcour-Min

For permission, serialization, condensation, adaptions, or for our catalog of other publications, write to Ozark Mountain Publishing, Inc., P.O. Box 754, Huntsville, AR 72740, ATTN: Permissions Department.

Library of Congress Cataloging-in-Publication Data

Delcour-Min, Paulinne – 1948 -
Spiritual Gold by Paulinne Delcour-Min

A book about past lives, but also about the future. We can make a difference and forge our destiny.

1. Reincarnation 2. Metaphysical 3. Past Lives 4. Jesus
I. Paulinne Delcour-Min, 1948 - II. Jesus III. Past Lives IV. Reincarnation V. Title

Library of Congress Catalog Card Number: 2018946277
ISBN: 9781940265544

Cover Art and Layout: www.vril8.com
Book set in:Calisto MT, Maiandra
Book Design: Tab Pillar
Published by:

PO Box 754, Huntsville, AR 72740
800-935-0045 or 479-738-2348; fax 479-738-2448

WWW.OZARKMT.COM
Printed in the United States of America

Back cover design: Original image by NASA, ESA and Jesus Maiz Apellaniz (Instituto de Astrofisica de Andelucia, Spain. Acknowledgment: David De Martin (ESA/Hubble). With the addition of the Holy Face image of Jesus based on the Turin Shroud (www.holyface.org.uk).

For Derrick Hastings Rowley

1922–2008

As we walked to Frodsham churchyard to put flowers on Granddad's grave you told me Granddad believed God had more sense than to stack up souls in heaven, *for all eternity*, after one brief outing. Granddad had believed in reincarnation.

I was ten, and it was as though you switched on a bright light in a darkened room. The passion for knowledge that was kindled on that summer's evening has led to this book.

Thank you, Dad, for everything.

If you would prosper in challenging times, this book is for you.

Making sense of the chaos in the world ...

BOOK 1

Spiritual Gold: Finding Your Compass for Life

Contents

Introduction
Who We Are

There have always been three big questions that have intrigued, puzzled, vexed, and haunted us down the ages.

Who are we?

Why are we here?

Life—what is it all about?

From the moment we first open our eyes, we find ourselves in a mysterious world. The mystery is so compelling that we can't help but search for answers. Who as a child has not looked at the stars and longed to unravel their riddles? And as adults we may become astronomers... or scientists... or doctors, because as long as we've been on this planet we've searched to unriddle the mystery of ourselves and the universe. And such has been our skill and determination that we have indeed come a long way by searching **outside** of ourselves for answers. But some of the answers lie **within**—and when we explore the deeper levels of our own consciousness we find that the answers to the big questions of life, like those above, are already there. The catch is, they are tantalizingly out of reach of the everyday logical mind operating in beta state, our problem-solving level of consciousness. We need to slip down into daydreamy alpha, and slide into the theta levels of lucid dreaming before we find the keys to unlock the deepest treasures of our minds. But when we do, nothing is hidden from those who know how to look.

And that's what has occupied me for over thirty years now. Looking! I always wanted to know more.

- I'd heard about people with memories of previous lifetimes.

- Read of mystics who had experienced being one with everything.

- I myself had an out-of-body experience (OBE) when I was fourteen,[1] so I knew from an early age that I was more than my body.

- Ever since a child I could sense things in old buildings—the psychic imprinting that happens over time.

So I'd always known there was more, that there were other less tangible levels to life. And I'd wanted to explore them. First, I used meditation, then as the years went by I went much further, because I utilized the deep inner work that's possible with past life therapy. I trained as a past life and soul therapist,[2] and found that if we wanted to know who we truly are, we have to go back to the beginning—the very beginning of everything, the Big Bang, when the universe began.

Science tells us,

According to Big Bang theory, all the matter that makes up you, me and everything in the universe was once condensed into a singularity and burst into existence at the same moment. If there were no limits to non-locality, this could mean that **we are all "entangled" at a quantum level**, that **we are all one consciousness** and that **"space" and our existence is just an illusion.**[3]

---

1 A loud noise frightened me half to death and I found myself on the ceiling, looking down at the scene. It only lasted a few seconds and I shot straight back into my body, but I never forgot; after that I knew I wasn't my body, I was the bit that had flipped out. The OBE had been instantaneous, and automatic, it just happened. It was at the time of the Cuban Missile Crisis, and there was much talk of "the four-minute warning" we would get before a nuclear attack reduced us to a radioactive cinder. A dreadfully loud sound in a building had made me literally jump out of my skin, because I'd mistaken it for the sirens of the nuclear warning.

2 Explained in detail in chapters 3–4.

3 From the science column in *The Metro* newspaper, November 19, 2010, published in England. "Nonlocality" is how physics describes the phenomena of action at a distance, when particles can be invisibly connected in a way that transcends space and time. NIST, the National Institute of Standards & Technology in America, as well as other institutions such as the University of Vienna in Austria, have conducted experiments that prove this, using photon pairs and fiber optic cables. Einstein called nonlocality "spooky action at a distance." Nature tends to limit the distance we perceive this action in operation, but in altered states of consciousness mystics have perceived the

Science, in this case theoretical quantum physics, offers an explanation for what mystics have known empirically throughout the ages: that we are all one—although we are separated out from each other by means of space and time. Space and time create the illusion of our individuality, but we are all still entangled at a quantum level. We are individual in the same way the cells in our brains are individual, if you will. And as the cells work for the majesty of a greater whole—that of facilitating *our* consciousness—indeed so do we. That is exactly what we are doing as we fulfill our incarnation's purpose by tasting and gathering the fruits of Creation. Now in our case the majesty of the greater whole for which we are working has many names:

The One,

The Divine,

Source,

All That Is,

The Creator,

God,

Great Spirit,

The Great Mystery

And as you know, there are many more names for God, but God doesn't mind which name we use, because what's more important than the name is **the intention with which we use it**, and that alone takes our words winging up through the dimensions of the universe to the Divine, like a dove going Home.

Our Home *is* in the spiritual world, our Home is in God. Our Home is God.

When we are here we are spiritual beings doing our best to live in matter.

We have set ourselves a very hard task.

It can appear that the material world is all there is.

---

original connection and have experienced being one with everything.

Here, we are not only separated from each other but also from our greater self, the part of us that gives rise to all our incarnations. And it's all too easy to stifle the quiet inner voice of intuition, thus gagging our angels and guides. We can deny God and try to reduce the world to what we can measure—but our psyche knows better, our soul remembers. We enter another territory when we dream each night. And it will always be our birthright to find safe passage Home when we leave our incarnation behind and our physical body dies. No matter what we've done, *eventually*[4] we will return to God and bathe in bliss—before we're sent out on another mission, that is! ...To have another crack at gathering the fruits of Creation and another go at developing and enriching our souls, *as we assist the Divine to transcend.*

I can remember being quite shocked when it was explained to me in meditation that God is a transcendent being... and that was why God had orchestrated the Big Bang and the subsequent wave of Creation that we are living in.[5] I'd assumed God was static and perfect, and thus beyond change. But not so. We are made in God's image (our spirits are), so we shouldn't really be surprised that God is as restless as we are for experiential enrichment. And that is our job—to provide enrichment for the Creator. That's why we are here. We are part of God, but we are the part that was sent out for this purpose. And ever since the universe began we have been drifting through its dimensions, incarnating here and there and gathering experiences... having lives, savoring existences, expressing consciousness in a myriad of ways. We are part of God's eyes and ears and senses in the evolving material world, in the universe... and we will be until we have nothing left to learn.

Since it's our job to incarnate, and we have done so many times before, let's look at how an individual incarnation begins. I am going to start by doing this—so that's chapter 1. I explain how I came to be me, how I came to do past lives, and I share the method by which I work, so you can see how a simple inner journey brings far memory recall. And in later chapters I'll share some of the most amazing regressions that have come up over the thirty years I've been working in this field—including past life memories of Jesus, which are the jewels in the book.

---

4 What has gone on in the life will influence the experiences in the spiritual world, and will be reflected in the choices and lessons for the lives that follow.

5 There have been Big Bangs before, and previous waves of Creation. Our current universe is not the first.

And let me be clear, all the lives I write about are mine. They have been chosen because of the treasures they hold. They are lives I have lived at different points in time, and they offer a good illustration of a soul's journey. With my passion for knowledge, coupled with access to countless regression sessions, the research part was comparatively easy. The hard part was actually living the lives! It's taken me ten thousand years and many deaths to gather the experiences I share in my books *Spiritual Gold*, *Holy Ice*, and *Divine Fire*; there can't be many people who have traced their soul's journey in such depth.

But the best place to start is in the here-and-now, with this, the life I am living in the present. The point of power always lies in the present. It is the anvil on which we forge our soul.

The following account is fact.

This is how my incarnation began.

Here are the secrets of time...

Chapter 1
Reincarnation: It's My Time to Be Born Again

When we come into a new life we bring our backstory with us. Not all of it, but enough to give our life its purpose. My problem was that long ago on Earth I'd made a promise. Perhaps it was foolish, but I'd made it with all my heart and soul, and so my heart energy had stamped it deep in my soul. I would have to redeem that promise.

But centuries passed.

I flowed through life after life. I was man, I was woman... as I wove my personal tapestry of experience through the medium of time. And after each outing into the universe, each foray into space and time, I returned Home, for a good rest in the peace of the Divine. It was like sleeping in a fluffy blanket of light, warm and safe in the Creator's heart. Sometimes it was so safe you did not want to go back out and chance another incarnation in the streams of time. And that's when a bit of persuasion was brought to bear.

It happened like this.

I was blissfully between incarnations.

I was held by a loving, living, warm light... in bliss... in peace... the peace that passes all understanding... and I was untroubled by any thoughts of a promise, or indeed by any thoughts at all. I wasn't *doing* anything, I was just *being, just pure Being.*

But angels and guides had clustered around me. They had come to take me into form, to take me into a body for a new life in the material world. I had to leave the realms of light and enter the universe again. Well, that's what they were saying.

The angels began to string me like a harp, connecting certain core memories and experiences with feelings... then they resonated the "strings," stirring memories, feelings, waking me up. They sang, not like we sing with words, but it was all vibration and pitch and glorious, like the music of the spheres. Their singing vibrated the strings; I'm being tuned in for what is to come: for a life.

This heavenly music is the music of incarnation.

Then the guides and angels surround me and detach me from the light, pulling me with them, still wrapped in living light. The light swirls around me and through me, weaving and creating a light body for me. This is what I become and what I travel in. We move down into the vibrations of the universe... down and down the dimensions... down until I am just above Earth.

I am in a body of living light with angels and guides.

I am neither male nor female, nor anything else. I am pure essence, not limited by any decision as yet.

The guides and angels continue, reminding me, stirring my conscience.

Saying it is time. Saying that I have things to do.

Reminding me of the promise.

Their dialogue continues as a collective voice in my mind.

I am reluctant but they aren't letting up.

"Of course, we could find someone else," they say. "If you don't honor your promise, you could be of service elsewhere, how about a nice spot in the desert? Sculpting the sand dunes again?" I'd done it before, they knew.[6] And long eons of aesthetic pleasure harnessing the wind beckoned... but then I remembered the loneliness. No, not again.

"I'll pass on that," I replied.

The promise? Now what was it? What had they said?

They were shaking their heads and saying, "Well, perhaps it's for the best. You don't always get it right, and it's rather important this time. We'll remind someone else instead. Now, how about..."

---

6 Since the earliest of times I've had an affinity with the devic beings that maintain the fabric of Creation. These maintenance entities include angels and nature spirits. It would be more accurate to call some of my experiences in the devic realms "existences" rather than incarnations.

They ran through other possibilities—but I wasn't really listening anymore—because I'd begun to recall the promise.

And I remembered.

It had been given freely, right enough, the promise. But two thousand years had slipped by, lives had come and gone, and I'd been busy... lost track. Busy, like we all are, busy developing and enriching our souls (for what else is the purpose of having life after life, if not that?), and it had slipped my mind. But it was when I remembered who I'd made it to, well, then, there was no going back.

"Let me do it," I pleaded. "I'm sorry, I forgot. I'll be diligent, work hard, get it right... I will. I will!"

Silently they considered.

Yes, the promise! How a few little words could suddenly mean so much. But then, it was **Jesus** they'd been given to. Not just to anyone, but to *Him*. I didn't want to let *Him* down, how could I? Not Jesus... no.

"Please let me do it, I'm ready now," I said with humility, and I was.

"Very well then," they said, and showed me the parents they had in mind.

I can tell that the father being considered would be loving and kind, and that the woman he had married has enough unhappiness to give me the wounds I need, were she to become my mother.

Wounds?

But from the perspective of the spiritual world this seems quite a reasonable idea, even a good one—it will make me more sensitive and keep ego in check—and I note she has a passionate belief in education, so in time I will learn how to heal my wounds and be able to help others heal theirs. Pity they hadn't married the right people, but then we don't always stick to our plans.

Memories of previous lifetimes with the father stir within my soul, and I grow more and more excited. I cry, "Yes! Oh, yes!" and effervesce to a fever pitch of ecstasy that plunges me into conception.

*But as I remember all this while lying on a therapist's couch—in a regression session—I can't help but wonder, **is this wise?** Knowing how things turn out,* *couldn't I have picked a different mother?*

But I had already plunged in, there was no turning back, and there I am: a tiny speck in the glorious cathedral that is my mother's womb.

The weeks and months pass.

The little bundle of cells that anchors the part of my consciousness that is in the material world grows ever more complex. The tiny body grows bigger. I weave in strengths and weaknesses so the body will be able to meet the lessons planned for my coming incarnation. At this stage I am still in the largeness of my being, still in touch with angels, guides, and the accumulated wisdom of my soul, with access to knowledge beyond our imaginings. Because only a tiny tip of that which I am has penetrated matter; but over the time of gestation, more and more of me telescopes down into the little body growing in the womb. This is going to be my spacesuit for life on planet Earth. It could *never* hold the largeness of my being, and that is not its purpose, but it will easily hold enough of me to undertake the coming incarnation. It will enable me to learn what I need from this venture down the frequencies of the universe.[7]

Time passes.

The womb, once so spacious, now feels tight and restricting. I slip in and out of the developing body and spend time in the energy field that surrounds my mother, what you would call her aura. She goes about her everyday life, and I begin to gain a sense of place. When in her aura I am aware of the streets and the houses, aware of the hill and the park where she walks. I hear conversations and I get a sense of the people around her.

---

7 "The largeness of my being" was the spontaneous term that came up in my regression. It refers to the particular cell in Source's brain (for want of a better way to put it) that gives rise to me, and is responsible for all my previous incarnations, and any parallel or future lives that may be going on.

Source gives rise to **all** our "largenesses of being." But all are connected, and there is a merging that is difficult to understand in our state of separation. Those wishing to know more of the structure of God will find much to think about in the books of Guy Steven Needler published by Ozark Mountain Publishing. As he says, at our present level of spiritual evolution we are building the tools to build the tools to begin to understand God, so the images and explanations we may receive in meditative communion with God can only take us as far as we can go at the moment. (See the diagrams in Figures 2 and 3 on pages 36 and 37.)

It is 1948, and World War 2 is over.

This is England.

The family I'm incarnating into live in the North West of England, in the lush agricultural county of Cheshire. It's the hill and the park of Frodsham I'm aware of—Frodsham being a sleepy little Cheshire village set between the marshlands of the Mersey estuary and the steep scarp slope of sandstone rock that forms Frodsham hill.

Winter turns into spring, and I prepare for the inevitable forgetting that birth will bring. When labor starts Mum is taken into hospital, and on a chilly March morning I enter a bleak postwar world. For the first time I feel cold. The shock of birth begins the forgetting, and I'm still cold when the hospital staff check me over—weigh me in old metal scales. It's a relief when I'm wrapped up and given back to Mum. Dad visits in the afternoon, and this is the day I see my parents' faces for the first time. I had visual awareness before, but it was sharper with the landscape than with people. They were more of an energy blur.

Some days later they take me home to their rooms above Granddad's and Grandma's jewelry shop in Frodsham. This is where Dad works. He's a watchmaker.

My parents met during the war.

Dad was in the Royal Air Force, and he'd been stationed in Belgium when he met my mother. So he's English and Mum is Belgian. When she married him she left home and country and came to England. I'm their first child. She'd been hoping for a boy, so I was a bit of a disappointment to her already, but she got her wish eighteen months later when my brother was born.

Very little happened in Frodsham.

The Thursday market in Main Street was the excitement of the week, and I remember Mum looking at the stalls, pushing my brother in a pram, and buying coral pink material to make me a party dress.

When I started school, a year seemed to stretch on forever.

But infant school gave way to junior school, and in those days, when you weren't actually in school, you were encouraged to play out. My friends and I would wander country lanes and roam the wild places in the park and on the hill. We followed the changes of the seasons, picked bluebells and blackberries, stuffed our pockets with conkers, admired raindrops strung out like jewels across spiders' webs fine as silk. We grew up close to the Earth in a way my own children never had the chance to. No one seemed to worry about stranger danger then.

The warm red and gold sandstone of the hill became an important part of my childhood. It was solid and comforting, like the bones of the Earth. Summers were spent scrambling over the dramatic rock formations, clinging on tightly to tufts of purple heather. We made dens in the bracken, climbed gnarled old oak trees—and sometimes our mothers took us up to the grassy slopes at the top for a picnic. If we were lucky we would be treated to slides down the helter-skelter, a curious structure that perched on the very top of the hill.

A favorite childhood game was cowboys and Indians. The rookery in the park was the best place to collect feathers for our arrows and headdresses—and I always wanted to be an Indian, but I didn't remember why.

Frodsham has a lovely old church. It is built from the local rock, and its very stones are steeped in history, some carved a thousand years ago in Anglo-Saxon times. Over the centuries it had been made bigger, but there were still original carvings to be seen in the vestry. With my friends I sang in the choir there, and I loved the atmosphere of ancient reverence. Being there was like touching the past, and it made me feel safe. Sunday Bible readings told of Jesus, and my eyes wandered to the stained-glass windows where vividly colored pictures of him and his disciples glowed with light. They fascinated me, and though there was a compelling reason, I no longer remembered why.

Walking home from choir practice on wintry evenings with my friends I would look up at the stars, intrigued by the mysterious constellations. Shining like beacons in the darkness of space they beckoned to me, and in answer I searched our local library for science fiction books ripe with stories set on other worlds. But I couldn't have explained, even to myself, why I found tales of living out there in the stars so appealing… I had well and truly forgotten who I was.

And things were never the same after my sister was born.

I was nearly eight when she was brought home from the same hospital where my brother and I had entered the world, and looking back it is easy to see that my poor mother was weighed down by postnatal depression.

In many ways the fifties were grim years, and Mum had brought her own emotional wounds with her when she came to England. She'd settled down and picked up the language easily enough, she spoke English, French, and Flemish, and it wasn't that she wanted to return to Belgium—indeed we spent every summer there, but she didn't find it easy to flow with life, and by the time I was in grammar school she had been hospitalized for manic depression. These days it is called bipolar disorder. She was given electroconvulsive shock treatment, which was brutal, and proved to be no solution really.

I loved Mum. She was pretty, bright, and charismatic. When you are little, your parents seem to be god-like beings. When I first discovered their mortality I can remember crying my eyes out at the very thought of Mum dying. I loved both Mum and Dad dearly, but there is a primal bond with the mother who suckles you and brings your body into the world. That she could be taken from me was the most awful possibility I had ever contemplated. That night I wept for both of them, but I have to confess the hottest tears were for Mum.

She had an animal magnetism and a warmth about her. She had a very strong personality, but when all that energy turned in on itself it was awesomely destructive. Although children are resilient and I was happy enough when out of the house playing, the rages and anger that were part and parcel of her depression were an inescapable part of my childhood. As a defense I began to develop an inner life and it became my refuge. I would daydream, and this would annoy Mum if she caught me. I was often scolded for it and accused of "wasting my time."

I daydreamed in school too and had to keep pulling myself back into the lessons, particularly during maths. Time and again I'd be gazing out of the window across the playing fields—where wicked winds blew across the estuary marshes to torment us when we were playing hockey—only to look round and find that the rest of the class had their heads down and were all busy writing.

I liked learning but I never enjoyed school.

Helsby was the next village along from Frodsham on the road to Chester, and it had the nearest grammar school—so that's where I'd been sent, and despite my daydreaming I did well, scooping the Runcorn prize for Arts for my A Level grades in English, art, and geography. But I was glad when my school days came to an end.

In geography I'd learned about rocks and the forces that shape landscapes, and I'd discovered that the stable sandstone of my childhood had been on adventures of its own. In previous world ages it had been part of a vast red dessert of sand dunes, and been under the sea when Britain was near where Africa is today. I think it's as well to know that what looks so solid can flux in the alchemy of time, and that a new world age can be so very different from the last.

In 1966 I left school and went to study in Manchester. The buzz of a big city was exciting.

Now, I'd loved dancing ever since I'd first seen the Beatles when they'd played at the dance hall on Frodsham hill,[8] and by the time I was in my last year at school I'd gone dancing most weekends. In Manchester I found I had the pick of lots of college dances to go to, and once I settled down I was very happy there.

Art was my subject, and ceramics became my main area of specialization, although we also worked with wood, and metals like silver, copper, and brass, and spent time in fine art. I did enjoy etching, I loved the smell of the resin on the steel plates, but I felt an affinity with clay. It was so receptive and immediate, it came alive in my hands, it spoke to me. I loved the way clay expressed itself by breaking into rough textures that reminded me of the landscape and rocks of my childhood, and when it was rubbed with metal oxides and dipped in engobes or glaze, the searing heat of the kiln transformed it and brought out its beauty. What I loved best was creating organic, flowing, hand-built forms.

My work was influenced by the curves of natural forms and Art Nouveau. Looking back now, I can see a link between my experiences in the devic realms and my artwork. It wasn't sand dunes I was working with here, but it *was* sandy textures of disintegration.

For my thesis I went to Spain to study the extraordinary architectural ceramics of Antonio Gaudi (1852–1926). As there are no straight lines in nature, Gaudi had declared that the straight line belonged to man, while the curved line belonged to God; this rendered the curved line superior, being the one favored by the Divine, and so he had constructed his buildings with structurally sound curves, utilizing hyperbolic parabolas and forms reminiscent of bones and vegetation. The organic

---

8 It had been the autumn of 1962, when I was fourteen. Being so near to Liverpool, all the Merseybeat groups came to play there. (The Mersey View dance hall, as it was called, was next to the helter skelter. Remember the Beatles' song *Helter Skelter*, released in 1968?)

quality of his work resonated with mine, and I adored his sinuous buildings clad in their joyful ceramic mosaics that celebrated life, the most famous being the temple of the Sagrada Familia in Barcelona.[9]

At the end of the course I was awarded a first-class honors degree in three-dimensional design, did a postgraduate teaching course, and became an art teacher in 1971.

The day I got my degree results Mum said I was a disappointment to her because I wasn't a doctor! But I'm far too squeamish for that to have been the faintest of possibilities, and I just had to laugh because it was so ludicrous. After watching me study art for years to come up with that out of the blue on the day I'd finished—well—it freed me from needing the approval of others. (That was quite a gift when you consider the sort of *X Files* territory my regression work would take me into later.) Mum had recently trained as a nurse and was enamored of all things medical, and if you remember, my parents had married the wrong people. As she would often say, she should have married the Belgian doctor she used to go cycling with before she met Dad, and she should not have listened to her interfering mother.

But it's easy to blame others. It's only when you take responsibility for your decisions that you can move on to a better place. Our lives are the sum total of all the decisions we have ever made—so if you don't like it, you need to draw up a plan of action to make changes. Mum was so headstrong I think she was being a bit disingenuous here, passing all the blame on to my grandma.

However, never let interfering people meddle with your destiny!

Following *your* interests and *your* passions will take you along the path *your* soul has mapped out for your incarnation—even though, at a conscious level, you will have forgotten what it is. What we hope to achieve will have slipped below the threshold of our conscious awareness, but there are always promptings to guide us, from our heart and subconscious, our guides and our angels. And for me, metaphysics and meditation became the next interests to pursue after art. When you think about it, meditation was a logical extension of my daydreaming, and as such, a result of the wounds I'd needed from poor Mum.

Meditation offered a means to explore unseen dimensions—those of the inner world and the world of the shaman. I studied yoga and

---

9 This and six of his other buildings were given world heritage status by UNESCO in 2005.

read whatever books I could find on these topics. I devoured Carlos Castaneda's books about his studies with Don Juan Matus, a Yaqui Indian shaman, and was riveted by his accounts of ventures into nonordinary reality.

I came across Rudolph Steiner's writings and found them full of fascinating information, and it was from him I learned that our personal guardian angels are angels of record, who record our lives to give God an accurate account when we die. But according to Steiner, unless we had formed a relationship with our angel while we were alive, we would not be able to hear what was being said; we would be deemed not to be interested. Well, true or not, this made me long to meet mine—I wanted to hear everything!

There is nothing mysterious or difficult about meditation.

The inner vision we use is the same as when we dream, and we do that effortlessly every night. You just need the luxury of a little quiet time to yourself.

Before settling down to meditate I made sure not to be disturbed. I lit a candle and some incense out of respect for the angels and to help them draw near. I made myself comfortable in a chair, closed my eyes, and prayed. I asked God for protection and help, and then I visualized light streaming down from God all around me, keeping me safe. I made a heartfelt request for what I hoped to achieve, and then I tried to still my mind and be receptive.

At first I sensed my angel as a ball of light. On later occasions I saw her as a small winged figure to my right-hand side, at shoulder height. In time I learned her name and as I got better at tuning into her she appeared larger.

But sometimes the unexpected happens.

One day I began a meditation and connected with my angel but found my awareness in space, passing the moon. I wondered what was going on. Should I pull my mind back to Earth or trust the angel? This dilemma was not what I was expecting at all.

Well, if you can't trust your guardian angel, who can you trust?

So I surrendered to the journey.

We alighted on the sun in the dimensions inhabited by angels. It was bright and very light, but there was no fire on that level. Graceful plumes of a fine, white, powdery sun dust shot up from the surface as we landed, and a tall white-robed angel greeted us and guided us into vast white caves filled with angelic choirs praising the Creator. I soon felt restless and asked if they ever got bored. With a gentle laugh he said that I did not understand angels to ask this, and that, no, they didn't. When we left them to their singing I stroked the soft feathers of his wings and asked our guide his name. The reply was "Michael," and in the instant I knew exactly who it was. I felt a bit taken aback to find I had been so flippant and familiar with an archangel, but he hadn't seemed to mind at all.

At that time all memories of meeting angels (including those you will find in later chapters) were well below the threshold of my conscious awareness, lost to me in the forgetting that had come with birth—but it was certainly a comfort to have met Michael, and an unexpected glimpse of spiritual gold.

If I hadn't read about angels in the Steiner book I might never have met Michael, and it is amazing how books can change your life. I got a lot of mine at the Mind Body Spirit festivals when they started up in London in the seventies. It was easy to get a train from Manchester to London, and each year I would visit, thirsty for knowledge, and on the hunt for more books.[10]

The festivals were exciting events; there were always new things to explore and just being with so many like-minded people was very affirming. There would be talks, workshops, demonstrations, and stands that sold crystals, Native American jewelry, flower remedies, relaxing music, essential oils, Kirlian photography (and later aura photography), and all manner of interesting things that you couldn't get hold of elsewhere. Here I came across spiritual healing, and the energy of Archangel Raphael began gently rippling into my life, for it is Raphael who is the archangel of healing.

---

10 One year I found a book on Findhorn, a community in Scotland where they worked with devic beings to grow phenomenal vegetables on very poor soil. It was very exciting and revolutionary, working with nature spirits, and over the years Findhorn has gone from strength to strength. They say they grow people there now, instead of cabbages, because it's a place for spiritual growth, where people flock from all over the world to do workshops and courses. I never dreamed one day I'd be invited to go there, to do some sessions for a facilitator who had seen me demonstrate in London, but that's what happened in 1988.

Unfortunately, by now it was too late to be of any help to Mum. After she'd raised me and my brother and sister, she'd left the world by her own hand.

It was the spring of 1976 when the burden of her depression crushed her in the end. Various contributing factors had collided. For health reasons she'd been told to give up smoking, which she was finding impossibly hard; we'd all flown the nest, so perhaps she felt we didn't need her anymore in the same way we used to, because my sister had just gone off to university and my brother and I were both married; and she was caught up in the middle of a house move. We can think we want something, and not realize how much we'll miss what we used to have. Change is scary. She'd never had a good word to say about the old house... but she never actually moved into the new one. It can't have been easy for Dad.

But in a situation like that you're always left asking yourself, "What could I have done to make things turn out differently?" and, "How could I have helped Mum more?" I was still seeking the answers, and that, coupled with a pull I felt deep inside, propelled me into healing.

Chapter 2
Kundalini and My Journey into Healing

There's a bit of a backstory with me and healing.

During my student days I had come across an article about healing in a Sunday newspaper. It was about "distant healing," so called because the healer does not need to be present. It was a very unusual topic to find in a newspaper, and it wasn't long before I had a go—with quite unexpected consequences.

A friend of my father's lived in Manchester with his wife. They had been best mates in the war, and were billeted together in the house where my father met my mother, my Belgian grandma's house. So they went back a long way, and Uncle Alf had always been very kind to me. When my mother was having a particularly bad time I would be sent to stay with Uncle Alf and Auntie Doris in the school holidays. They had no children of their own, and always made a fuss of me, and they kept an eye out for me when I was a student in Manchester. Uncle Alf became ill and was in hospital. I'd just read the article, and for several nights before I went to sleep I tried to do what was suggested. I imagined flying over the rooftops to be with him in hospital, covering him in light and thoughts of healing, giving him strength. And then flying back. It was simple enough.

Well, he did get better and came home—and who knows, perhaps I helped—but the strangest thing happened on the last night. I was ready for sleep, lying relaxed when I had the sensation of fire rushing up my spine. I could see it in my mind's eye, silvery-gold flames, but no heat. I found I could breathe into this and push it in pulses up my spine until the flames were coming out of my crown. I'd never had anything like this happen to me before, and after what must have been at least ten minutes it stopped, only to start again after a short break. Exactly the same thing happened again, so there were two bursts of this fire, both of equal length.

I didn't feel any different the next day. I got on with my work with clay, hand building the organic forms of my heavily textured pottery, but after that I began to tune into clay differently. With my inner ear I could hear its sound, a sort of primordial resonance. Clay is rotted rock, rock digested by the forces of nature—and strange to say, it was as if a deep cave belched.

The "fire" never happened again, and at the time I had no idea what the experience was about. (I can't lay any claims to having helped my mum with this type of healing either.)

Years later I read about Kundalini.

I found that we carry an energy like two serpents in our spine, coiled up at the base. When this energy is awakened it surges up the spine, crossing over itself and entwining at the energy centers in the body known as the chakras; it emerges as tongues of fire at the crown. Indeed these serpents are depicted on the caduceus, the ancient symbol of the healer which is familiar to every doctor even today. In fact it is not really a symbol at all, but rather an accurate depiction of our subtle energy body.

So I guess my healing intentions activated this energy, causing it to rise, and the breathing was to pulse it through the slight resistance of the chakras.

I must have had attainments garnered in previous lives that only needed to be triggered, because people work at this for years, often with no results. There is a whole system of yoga called Kundalini yoga. But from what I've read it is never wise to force it. The Kundalini will rise when you are ready. It was just a very strange thing at the time, and not something I talked about. The only friend I confided in had no idea what it was.

The staff symbolizes our spine, and the serpents cross through the chakra points. The wings symbolize your mind being able to take wing and fly up to God through the opened gate of your crown chakra. The crown chakra is represented by the circle at the top of the staff.

We do actually have a neat little pair of white wings above our temples in the subtle energy body. Some people's are still budding, as yet unfurled. I saw mine during my first soul therapy session in the 1980s. (Soul therapy is explained in the next chapter.)

The caduceus is sometimes called **The Staff of Hermes**. Hermes was **the messenger of the gods**.

The Caduceus

But time had moved on, and it was now the early 1980s, not 1969 as it had been when I was a student. More than ten years had passed, and it was time to find out about healing properly. As I said, when I'd seen demonstrations at the Mind Body Spirit festivals I'd really felt a pull, an almost physical sensation. But what clinched it was a random choice to have a Kirlian photograph taken at one of the festivals.

The early 1980s had not been good years for me. This was an unhappy time in my life. After my mother died my first marriage had ended, and in 1980 I'd got caught up with a new partner's business venture that seemed to leak money. For several years it had sucked up all my time and energy. The photograph promised to capture the etheric energy field of my hands, revealing where my energy was strong and where it was weak, or even where the pattern was broken—and I was told that the significance of the patterns would be explained to me.

I was very curious.

After the photo was taken, a young woman gave me my one-to-one explanation. As she traced the meaning of the emanations from the different fingers of both hands, she came to the middle fingers. She said they showed my creativity was blocked—and I just burst into tears, *because it was*—and for a complete stranger to tell me this out of the blue took me by surprise. My creativity had always been my most precious gift, and taken for granted, but the situation I was in was all consuming, and I hadn't given it a thought. I was right off my true path and trapped both emotionally and financially.

As I wiped away my tears, she gently put her hands on me and calmed me down. After I'd dabbed the last tear she told me I had the gift of healing, and that I could communicate it to others. Something to do with the patterns around both little fingers…

But as soon as she said it, I knew she was right.

She said she'd given me healing when her hands were upon me, and now she suggested I join the National Federation of Spiritual Healers (NFSH), in order to develop my own gift as a healer.[11] She herself was a member—but first she said I had to get out of the situation I was in, and put my life in order, before I could think about helping others.

Well, I took her advice.

I extricated myself from the business.

I joined the NFSH.

---

11 I think we all have the gift.

Nowadays the NFSH is called **The Healing Trust** and it is a registered charity. Founded in 1954 it is the largest and oldest membership organization of spiritual healers in the UK. "Spiritual" is from the Latin "spiritus," meaning "breath of life." They define healing as **regaining the balance of mind, body and/or emotions**, and describe it as a natural energy therapy that complements conventional medicine by treating the whole person—mind, body, and spirit. Their healers are thought to act as a conduit for healing energy, the benefits of which can be felt on many levels, including the physical.

And that meant I was about to find out a whole lot more about such subtle energies as those pictured in the Caduceus.

Attending the courses of the National Federation of Spiritual Healers in 1984 was like finding the gateway into the world of subtle energies. We learned about the nonphysical bodies, chakras, and the levels and colors of the aura, because disease so often has its beginnings in the higher bodies before it manifests in the physical. There are medical intuitives like Caroline Myss and Lilla Bek who can see this, and Lilla was one of the main teachers. She is an internationally recognized spiritual healer, yoga teacher, and writer whose first book about the subtle energies was called *What Colour Are You?* This was published in 1980 and written in collaboration with Annie Wilson of the World Health Organization.

From Lilla I learned that we are literally "rainbow beings of light," because our higher energy bodies interpenetrate our physical body through the chakras. "Chakra" is an ancient Sanskrit word to describe these energy focal points, which when we are healthy spin like wheels radiating colors of light. The chakra at the base of our spine has a red color when it is functioning properly, but the color muddies and darkens if the chakra is blocked—perhaps by fear and anger, or by karmic debris, for example. We have seven of these chakra points, all the way from the base up to the crown of our head, and these correspond to the seven colors of the rainbow: orange is the color of the one just below the navel, yellow radiates out from the solar plexus, green is the heart color, blue for the throat, indigo for the brow chakra (which is the "third eye" through which we have our inner vision in meditation and dreams), and purple for our crown chakra, through which we open to the universe, to divine love, to God. As we continue to evolve we will activate the chakras beyond the crown, the next being the Alta Major. I've experienced its colors as being magnetic silver and radiant gold, although traditionally it is linked to magenta and peach. The sun disc above the heads of Egyptian deities like Isis and Hathor depicts this chakra. In the inner world I've had it described to me as "the crucible of transformation." Because it's where we can do alchemy, where we can turn debased energies back into their pure state.

Spiritual healing is the "laying on of hands," although touch is **not** essential and it works just as well if your hands are above the body, in the energy fields of the aura that surrounds the physical body. It can also be done by focused thought at a distance—distant healing—or by the healing power of prayer. Healing is one of the gifts of the Holy Spirit written about in the Bible, and was common practice in the early Christian Church. It is still practiced today in some churches (although you don't need any religious affiliation to do it; just the right intention).

The ability to heal is part of our nature. As Lilla Bek said, every parent who kisses a child's injury better is instinctively healing. Compassion opens the heart and then the healer is a conduit for the energy of the universe—I think of it as divine love—to flow through them to the healee. We have little heart chakras in the palms of our hands, and healers' hands often grow hot or tingle as the energy passes through. At the very least, healing brings peace as the healee is realigned with the harmony of higher levels of their being. Miracles can happen, but the outcome depends on the karmic situation and not just the healer. The healee has to be ready to let the condition go because they, or their loved ones, have learned the lesson it brings, even if it's something as simple as a change in values.

During a healing, usually the healee is seated. A stool is good, so there is access to their spine, or they could sit across a chair. You stand behind them with your hands lightly resting on their shoulders, and then it's like going into prayer mode: eyes shut, you lift your thoughts up to God, pull the light down, and surround yourself and the healee in light. Then it's a case of "Thy will be done." *You* do not *will* an outcome. (This is interference, and it will deplete your energy. You would simply be draining your own solar plexus, instead of using universal energy. It would be dangerous for your health, and also be karmically irresponsible.) Instead you let the energy flow through you without conditioning the outcome. The energy is self-intelligent; it flows where it's needed, and your intuition will tell you where to direct it through your hands as you gently move them just above the body. The highest good for the healee could be a swifter passing with less pain, or anything up to and including an amazing recovery. But at the very least it will bring peace. And, as a residue of the energy stays with you, you should feel lifted too.

Having merged your energy fields for the healing, when you finish you need to visualize separating out. For distant healing you would send the light and love out to a person (or situation) by asking the angels to take it and use it for the highest good. Plus you could ask for it to be multiplied by as many karmic dispensations as possible, which is particularly worth trying when attempting the healing of a situation—

like a war zone, say—as this could enhance the effect, and it's always worth a try. As they say in the North East of England where I live now, "Shy bairns get nowt" (shy children get nothing). No harm in asking! Angels respect our free will. They need to be asked.

***

One of Mum's gifts to me was to show me the absolute futility and addictive nature of negative thinking, and to demonstrate how we can manifest experiences and affect our future with our thoughts. She gave an absolute master class in this, poor Mum, and because thoughts are so powerful, I've learned that working with them in a positive way— through affirmations and visualizations—or just through being aware of them and switching tack when necessary, we can bring healing into our lives. We can be masters of our destiny, not slaves to negativity.

Living in the past and blaming others pulls us down into depression because the energy of the past moves much more slowly than that of the present. So it is depressing to dwell there in your mind. The energy of the future moves too fast for us to be comfortable, and so we feel worn out and stressed when dealing with planning ahead. Peace belongs in the present and that is where we find it. Pulling ourselves back into the present is always one of the greatest gifts we can give ourselves. Enjoying the moment, experiencing life through our senses, being aware of our breath, experiencing beauty, all these simple things free us from the cloying embrace of the past. Being in the moment without shouldering the heavy burden of the baggage from the past— there lies contentment.

Counting your blessings in the power of the present can help to reboot your thinking. It is simple and costs nothing. A change in attitude can make all the difference to your experience of life, and it does make sense when you think about it.

Even as a child I could see that what Mum was doing was the wrong way to go about things. Sitting chain smoking cigarettes, while heaping negativity on top of negativity was not making her happy. When I was teaching she said she wished she could see life through my eyes, and I really tried to show her. I should have liked her to have seen her grandchildren when they came along, and perhaps if I'd found healing earlier I might have had more success.

Healing had a profound effect on me. I felt I'd come home.

To help me develop as a healer the National Federation put me in touch with Naomi Long, a remarkable old lady who lived near me in Manchester. Naomi had been Bernard Leach's healer during the years she lived in Cornwall. I was most impressed by this because he was such an important figure in the world of ceramics. He had brought the techniques of the East over to Britain in the 1920s, and he was a great formative influence on the course of studio ceramics. His name had often come up in my studies.[12]

Healing opened me up, activated my chakras, and made me very sensitive to energies for a time. If I stood near a TV set I felt as though I was being rubbed down with sandpaper! Those shops with banks of TVs for sale were a nightmare. But this did wear off.

On some of my visits to Naomi there were other people there too.

I remember one nice young couple who were budding healers about to go to South Africa, and on another occasion a middle-aged man had come to see Naomi. She said to me, "Find his pain"—and that really put me on the spot! I had to scan him with my hands to find which area of his body was attracting the healing energy. But usually I met Naomi every couple of weeks, and it would just be the two of us. I practiced healing with her, and she often lent me spiritual books.

In England healing is unregulated.

An organization like the NFSH sets out standards of conduct and professionalism for its healer members, but there is nothing to stop someone just going ahead and doing whatever they want. So, as in all things in life, it is buyer beware even when it comes down to healing... and I was about to learn more than I wanted from one of this other type of healer.

Although this healer was not a Manchester-based man, one of his students had come to Naomi on a quest for knowledge.

---

12 Bernard Leach died in 1979, and it was after that Naomi came to Manchester.

Mr. Leach had been born in Hong Kong in 1887, but because his mother died in childbirth his maternal grandparents took him to live with them in Japan. They arranged for him to be schooled in England, and throughout his life he did much traveling between England and Japan.

In 1920, together with his friend Hamada Shoji, he founded a studio pottery in St. Ives, Cornwall. He is widely regarded as being the most important and influential artist-potter of the twentieth century.

In the study session with Naomi that evening we had it explained to us that the Earth had a band of dark energy around it called the "psychic layer." Above this was the spiritual world, and to reach it sometimes we had to break through the psychic layer. This dark energy was comprised of negative thought forms, perhaps traces of evil and black magic, the dross of the noetic world—and little did I know, but I was about to encounter it—that very night!

The student gave me a lift home.

But meeting this man's student had triggered something in me.

At the time I had no idea they'd awakened some unpleasant energies from a previous lifetime... and that the energies were seeking healing. In this earlier life I had been made a black magic sacrifice by a coven. I'd been given bracelets to wear that unbeknown to me had been charged on a black altar, and those who I thought were my friends had admired them and encouraged me to wear them. But as I wore them their energy turned the etheric energy in my blood to a nasty black. It was a bad death, what with the betrayal and the black magic and the taint in my blood. Blood is significant. It is not a trivial substance.

Well. That night as I lay in bed and looked around me, the door frame seemed to be rippling and melting in a truly sinister fashion. Something bad was happening and I was terrified. I shook uncontrollably with fear. I prayed harder than I ever have in all my life. After a while I could smell wafts of my mother's perfume and it comforted me. (Our departed loved ones may be in the other world but they still care, and they can draw close. Scent is often used as a communication bridge.)

Eventually I slept, and in the morning I awoke to an intense awareness of all the magic and evil in the area. This persisted for a few days and only abated when I realized that I had contacted the psychic layer. The realization broke the spell. (It was only considerably later when I had access to regression that I discovered the full story.) Meeting the man's student had raked it all up. My subconscious was trying to protect me, trying to warn me of the danger I might be in *because the last time I'd encountered energy like that I'd died horribly.* Obviously things were different now, and there was no danger, but to the subconscious mind hundreds of years ago might just as well have been yesterday. The subconscious isn't really aware of time.

Over the years I have met two other people who had similar experiences with the psychic layer, lasting a weekend in one case and a week in another. It's the overwhelming awareness of evil that is the clue. Normally we're screened from it by the energies of the world, the energies of daily life.

But as I didn't realize the connection between my frightful experience and the student, I did go along with them and a group of their student-healer-friends to one of the other healer's meetings. They took me with them, and I actually met the man himself.

The meeting was held in a hall with a small stage and a bar selling drinks. There must have been more than fifty people there. People he had helped, long-term healees, admirers, and fans. We sat around tables, each of us with a drink, chatting, while the healer moved from table to table greeting people. He had a glass of beer in one hand and a cigarette in the other!

The climax of the evening was the healing itself.

To the music that always opened Elvis's concerts he came on stage.

He stood, raised his hands, and moved through a series of postures that indicated he was directing healing energy to his followers who had prostrated themselves on the floor in front of the stage. His helpers, including the student-healers who brought me, moved along the rows of bodies, touching people, conveying healing. I had never seen anything like it!

Remember, I was new to healing. It was a very intense period in my life. I was very excited about healing and its possibilities, excited about higher dimensions and subtle energies, but that evening I had the inescapable feeling that this was a test. The feeling of being tested had begun to grow as soon as I got there. As we sat around with our drinks waiting for the healer to pass by our table and greet us, the palms of my hands had begun to tingle, which I tried to ignore... but instead of fading away, the tingling that heralded healing energy coming through me to heal someone only increased. Much as I tried to fight it I knew I, who had only just started, had to offer the great man healing. My palms were burning and tingling with energy that was being sent for him from the higher levels. I tried to ignore it, hoping it would go away. It only got stronger. My head felt strange, energy was fizzing, and I could feel something almost tangible there, at the back of my head.

I tell you if I'd had second sight that night I'd have expected to see a nimbus, a halo, there.

As the healer walked around chatting to people before he started, I shyly went up and explained about my hands and offered him the healing energy.

He said, "Give it to someone who needs it."

He turned the gift down.

But I think I passed the test, because the following evening I had a strange experience. My bedroom filled with a wonderful spiritual fragrance. It had no earthly source. I can only describe it as the scent of angels. (I came to know this as "the odor of sanctity," and had other experiences with it too.) It welled up in several places in my room. I walked about trying to locate the cause of the scent. It was like lilies and roses... and something else. Beautiful! It got so strong at one point that I had to leave the room. My sister (who was living with me at the time) actually noticed it before I did, and she asked me what it was. To this day I don't know, but I think it was a reward for doing what I didn't want to do: honoring the gift of healing and offering it to that man.

And as it turned out, he was dead within a year, which was surprising, because he was by no means old.

(In the regression it felt like he was the one who had actually killed me, the leader of the coven, so maybe there was some karma working out there. Like I had to forgive him, so perhaps symbolically this was achieved by the offer of healing.) I will never really know, because I must point out you can only ever *truthfully* say, "Someone *who felt like* X, Y, or Z did this to me." It is something for you to know, that might be helpful in explaining things, and it would certainly explain the crazy energies around my meeting these people in my present life. But whether we like it or not, we are all on a journey to wholeness and healing—so without any prompting from us life will provide opportunities for change. When we encounter certain energies things awaken, but it may not be *exactly* the same energies, just as we are not exactly the same personalities every time we incarnate. The universe is fluid, but patterns resonate. The resonance is what stirs up the energies. And no doubt I'd done something in an even earlier life to warrant that death! You could take it as a sign of spiritual evolution that the coven was now into healing...

However, the healer was nothing like an NFSH healer, and nor were his methods. But I have to thank him for giving me that opportunity, God rest his soul.

The spiritual path can bring strange experiences.

It can be a lonely one too.

At this time I was in the emotional wasteland between my two marriages.

***

So as you've seen there are two types of healing. In one you channel higher forces, in the other you use your own energy and deplete your solar plexus. The first is true spiritual healing, the second is what Naomi called "magnetic" healing, which happens if you *will* the person to get better. (There are no magnets involved!) Magnetic healing can be dangerous to the healer. Channeling higher forces actually benefits you, because a little residue remains within you. Naomi was very clear on this. So in spiritual healing we open our hearts to the loving, self-intelligent energy of the universe—God's love if you like—which when called forth flows down from the higher levels to restore our physical and spiritual harmony. This is what activates true healing. When we *will* healing, it's all mind and solar plexus. Perhaps the other healer simply burned himself out.

***

Naomi encouraged me to go on National Federation courses, even to join the regional committee. I went to the annual conference where the author Alan Young gave a talk I will never forget.

Alan talked of clients who responded to his treatments but then repeatedly slipped back into their old condition, making him feel as if he was endlessly mopping up water while somewhere the tap was still running. To his surprise the search for the tap often took his clients back well beyond their childhood to a previous lifetime, and they finally got better when they understood how the earlier life related to their present one. For example, one man's severe headaches had been linked to having his head literally severed from his body. He had had several lives where he had been beheaded one way or another.

I could understand this and I thought it a really intriguing idea.

The concept of reincarnation had made a lot of sense to me for a very long time, but I'd never done more than read about it. The problem was that the books I'd read always used material gathered through hypnosis, and from what I'd seen of stage hypnotists on the television I definitely did *not* want to be hypnotized. It saddened me to think I would never be able to find out about my own past lives—if, indeed, I'd had any. To this day I'm convinced the angels had a hand in what happened next.

Chapter 3
Past Lives, Soul Therapy, and Angels

By now it was 1985, and wishing to take my interest in healing further, I came to London to visit the Healing Arts exhibition. I wanted to learn a therapy, and was searching for the right one. I was looking for a way to combine healing with earning a living, and as I looked around the stands and picked out which talks I wanted to go to from the program, I noticed Dr. Francesca Rossetti was speaking on regression therapy. The program said this was working with past lives *without* hypnosis. Could this be what I was looking for?

I made sure I was there.

Like Alan, Francesca had found that our problems could stem from previous lifetimes, and she said much of our suffering was unnecessary because the past could be healed. She explained that she had studied with native healers in the United States and Japan, and had used what she'd learned from their shamanic ways of working for regression, and for what she called her **Pre-Creation Soul Therapy**.

The soul therapy involved:

- Shamanic journeying to the Source (God), before Creation!

- Working with angels!

- Using medicine rattles and sacred sounds from Native American traditions, for the releasing of karmic blockages and negative energies from the past that were holding us back.

Regression would give us the stories of our past lives, and soul therapy would heal and release any unwanted karmic detritus that was still affecting us now. She made it sound both profound and exciting. The journey into the inner world sounded fun. I'd found what I was looking for—someone who could let me see my own past lives without my being hypnotized—and once I started having my own experiences of the therapy I was hooked. I was to spend the next seven years studying and experiencing the work. And perhaps it was my many Native American past lives that made me feel comfortable with it, but I took to it like a duck to water.

After the exhibition, Francesca started training would-be therapists.

I sent my deposit for the training, but unfortunately before the first workshop something happened that was to plunge me into a personal crisis. When I explained what had happened, Francesca returned the deposit. Everything would have to wait.

***

It was Naomi. She went into hospital for a hip replacement operation and did not come out alive.

She was estranged from her daughter, who lived some distance away. She expressly did not want her daughter to visit her in hospital, but asked me to visit to give her healing. I was delighted to do this as she had been very kind to me. But things do not always go as we plan.

There were complications after the operation.

Naomi was in a lot of pain.

She couldn't get comfortable, no matter how the pillows were arranged, and then gangrene set in. I seem to remember being told they had nicked her bowel and accidently perforated it during the operation. (There was no culture of litigation back then. Accidents happen.)

This took days to play out, and I visited each day.

However, I had just come back from an NFSH event—with a new idea.

The speakers had been interesting, but in the lunch break, if we were keen, we could opt for extra one-to-one training with an established healer member. I jumped at the chance! I was fascinated with this new dimension of life and hungry for knowledge.

One of those giving this extra training was a lady who had spoken of her experiences in the war. She had lived through the bombing of Dresden, in Germany, during World War II. In one night the city was utterly destroyed but she had survived, because she was led by angels from building to building. She said it was only by the help of the angels that she'd threaded her way through the carnage and fire storm to safety. And as luck would have it, I was able to work with her.

It was an interesting lunch break.

When she'd finished the healing on our volunteer healee she did something I'd not come across before.

She closed the chakras by visualizing a symbol on them. A cross in a circle; and she encouraged me to do this. Innocent enough you might think. (In fact, it is the symbol for the Earth and the element earth in esoteric circles.)

So I'd learned something new. And when I was helping Naomi I added this in to what she had taught me to do. But what with one thing and another I never got around to discussing it with her. She trusted the NFSH, so did I, and I had no reason to doubt the lady blessed by angels.

When things got serious the hospital informed Naomi's next of kin. This was her daughter. Naomi had not told her daughter she was even going into hospital.

Her daughter came, and the next time I visited she was waiting for me. I was intercepted at the ward doors and sent away without seeing Naomi, and I was forbidden from visiting her ever again. As you can imagine, I was most upset. I'd never been told what the matter was between them, and I never did find out.

Naomi died, and I was not invited to her funeral.[13] In fact, I was told to stay away.

I never had the chance to say goodbye to her.

But having forbidden my attendance at the funeral, her daughter rang my doorbell and paid me a visit.

I invited her in.

Somehow she knew I'd used symbols in my healing. I hadn't told a soul, I'd had no reason to, so I was shocked by this and she had my full attention. She went on to say that symbols were dangerous because they opened up pathways in the mind. Who knows what temple training

13 This was October 1985.

we've had in previous lifetimes? What energies we've dabbled in? And I had to promise to stay away from symbols. She made me visualize a door in my mind being closed, locked and guarded by Archangel Michael. I tell you I was very shaken by this bolt from the blue. Perhaps she was clairvoyant, or perhaps she channeled the information—but somehow she had known. She said her mother had occult enemies, and they had been able to attack her through me. Without actually saying it she was accusing me of killing her mother.

She sat in my kitchen and pointed at a little glass pyramid-shaped prism on my table, the type with rainbow colors. It was an ornament, a gift I'd been given for my birthday. (It wasn't something I'd chosen.) She declared it a focus for bad energy, put her hand on the point, and said, "Can't you feel it?" It was only a couple of inches high. I had to take her word for it.

The next day I was bringing some food shopping home, and by now I had contacted my anger about the situation. I was cross to be excluded from Naomi's funeral and furious with her daughter. "She's not half the woman her mother was," I thought—when the carton of milk I was carrying was dashed from my hand. It spilt in the street, and I watched a white stain spreading on the pavement as I realized I was wrong. Naomi's daughter was a very powerful woman indeed. But one I never want to meet again.

***

The whole experience left me shocked, shaken to the core, and traumatized. Had I unwittingly caused Naomi harm? The very last thing I ever intended was that. I felt so bad I questioned everything. I threw out, or gave away, anything with a symbol on it; the little glass pyramid went to the bottom of the River Mersey nearby, and I prayed very hard. Meditating in my distress I was given words to comfort me that I cherished. For years I kept them carefully written on a piece of paper under my mattress, ready for any crisis. I don't know where that prayer is now after our house move, but I'm sure it's somewhere safe, and that I will find it one day—but what I'm really hoping is that I'll never need to use it again!

I had been plunged into the dark night of the soul and no mistake.

I was in no shape to start training with Francesca.

It took a long time to recover from that. In fact, I still find it very unsettling to write about, even now. I'd lost some innocence along the way, and I took a step back from healing. It is probably the main reason I didn't feel my future lay in that direction—that it was a road I'd personally come to the end of. And of course I've been very wary of symbols ever since. Hence I never got into Reiki, although a lot people who do healing do that. It just isn't for me because of the symbols. Oh! I'd really got my fingers burned there.

This healing chapter in my life had been a time of light and dark.

I only told a few close friends who were concerned because I looked so upset, but looking back now I should have told people in the NFSH. They would have had more experience than I had, and perhaps tools to get at the truth. When you've been abused you feel guilty, you don't want to talk about it, which is why abusers in the wider world so often get away with it.

Had it simply been an everyday accident with tragic results?

And a jealous daughter?

I don't know, but I dropped out of the regional committee.

However, life goes on.

***

One day there was an advert in the local paper that caught my eye.

The Christian Community in Manchester was advertising a talk about Revelations—you know, the section at the back of the Bible called *The Revelation of St. John the Divine.* I'd long pondered the mysterious words and images in those pages, and I have a sneaking feeling we are working through the prophecies today. My English grandfather, who died when I was six months old, was always intrigued by them, so I felt they must be important. I wanted to know more.

I went along to the address in the advertisement and found an ordinary house in South Manchester, very near where I lived. The church was the ground floor of the house. It was a small church, but it was part of a large organization and the Christian Community is possibly the only Christian Church that officially believes in reincarnation. It is in existence because of the work of Rudolph Steiner—the very same man whose books had caused me to meet my guardian angel. Sometimes it's a very small world.[14]

I wasn't much wiser after the talk, but the people were very welcoming and I attended services there, and eventually it did help me to move on with my life. Time is a great healer, as they say, and it is true ... and I began to yearn again to follow my passion to explore past lives.

***

When I was ready I contacted Francesca and arranged to study with her on the next course.

***

The best part of a year had passed, but when the time came I took four beeswax candles along as a gift to my first training weekend. Beeswax are the finest candles you can offer to God. They burned brightly on the therapy couch in the center of the room as we started the weekend with a meditation. Francesca talked about the angels we were going to work with. She explained that this would be:

- *Archangel Michael*—our guardian and protector

- *Archangel Uriel*—angel of truth, because without truth you can't build anything lasting

- *Archangel Gabriel*—angel of love

- *Archangel Raphael*—angel of healing.

In the meditation she invited the angels to join us. Being curious, I wondered if they'd come, and as we meditated I focused my awareness to find out.

In each corner of the room there was a tall winged figure, semitransparent, but with a strong outline, giving—what very definitely looked like angels—a very linear quality. They were leaning in toward the center of the room at a 45-degree angle, and the only thing that differentiated them was the symbolic object each carried. One had a sword, one an opened book, one a pyramid of softly twinkling, six-pointed, silvery-gray stars, and the fourth held a staff.

---

14 Steiner was born in 1861 and died in 1925. He was an Austrian philosopher, scientist, esotericist, and the most significant occultist of the last century. He wrote over 330 books, founded Biodynamic Agriculture, Waldorf Education, and the Anthroposophical Society. He is described as a multifaceted genius.

I knew Michael was traditionally depicted with a sword, although I'd not seen one when I met him. I guessed Raphael to have the staff because it called to mind the staff at the center of the caduceus (the ancient symbol for healing). I made another guess, that it was Gabriel holding the stars, because they looked strangely magnetic and love is a magnet that draws people together. Purely by default that left Uriel to be the one with the book. So although I wasn't certain who was who, I did have an answer. The angels had come.

Once back home, I searched through books of angel paintings to find artists who had perceived them as I had. The closest match was the eighteenth-century visionary William Blake (1757–1827). His angels in the painting *Angels hovering over the body of Christ in the Sepulchre* were identical, apart from being empty-handed. You can see them in the illustration on the next page.

Confirmation about Uriel came later, when a friend gave me Allegra Taylor's book *I Fly Out with Bright Feathers*. Here it says Uriel carries the Book of Truth and the first page is a mirror. But as he was facing me, all I saw was the back of the book.

A very curious thing about the weekend was the venue.

It should have been held at Francesca's home, but at the last minute she'd had to book a much larger room—and at such short notice the only one available was in the local sports and leisure center. Believe it or not, we had just spent the entire weekend at the Angel Centre on Angel Lane, Tonbridge. Sometimes truth is stranger than fiction, and I think the angels were having a laugh!

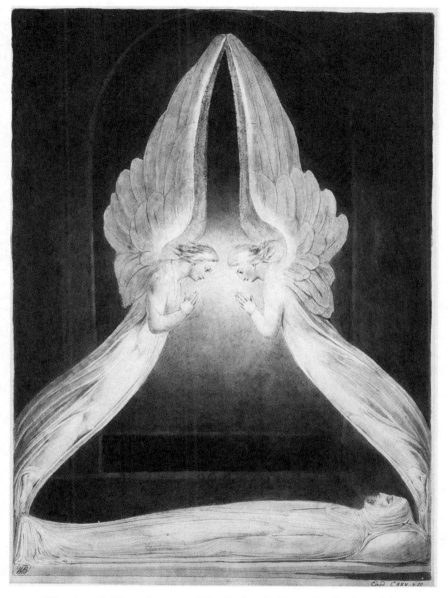

The Angels Hovering over The Body of Christ in the Sepulchre

by William Blake. England, late 18th century

© Victoria and Albert Museum, London.

Archangel Michael

In Cairo, Egypt, there is an ancient Coptic Christian church built over the site where the holy family sheltered when they fled from Herod. This was where Mary and Joseph took the baby Jesus until it was safe to return to Nazareth, and the small church that now stands on the spot has a remarkable atmosphere.

It holds saints' relics, and when I was there I was moved to tears by the energy of the place. One particular painting made a great impression on me. It was only small, but against a background of the most beautiful heavenly blue, scattered with golden stars, it depicted Archangel Michael slaying a dragon with a spear. As we left the church I knew I had to do a picture of him capturing the same feeling.

The illustration opposite is the result. Although I was limited to sharing it with you in black and white here, it conveys the essence of Michael, and you can see it in full color on my website: www.paulinnedelcour-min.com

The trip to Egypt had taken place many years after meeting Michael, but when I returned home I meditated and asked him how he wanted to be depicted. The answer that came was very fire themed. Against a blue and starry background he wanted to be seen holding a golden sword with a blade of fire, his hair like the sun's corona. A sun was to blaze from the hilt of his sword, which would be held against the fire of his solar plexus, and even the folds of the garment around his neck were to radiate out like flames.

I gave his upper body a solidness to communicate strength, but created a more transparent quality to the lower body to indicate the interdimensional nature of such a being. This picture is something of a dress portrait, like we have of our Queen Elizabeth in England, wearing her state robes and crown. It is not what she always wears, and it is the same with Michael. When I have met him in meditation he has been much more simply dressed. But he is the agent of God, his home is the sun, and were he to be flying directly toward you, head first, arrayed as I have depicted him and with his sword held high above his head and pointing at you, he would look like a mighty sun bearing down upon you, a series of concentric circles of fire, an embodiment of the sun. Michael fights on the side of Light in the cosmic battle between good and evil, and this is him as a radiant being, ready to be called.

Angels live outside of time, and so they can be in many places at what we regard as the same moment. Because of this they can work with many people at once. Michael is a very popular angel with many fans worldwide, but he always has time for you if you have an attitude of respect and a sincere heart. We can call on him for help and protection, and if karma allows it, miracles can happen.

Meditation is a wonderful tool to enhance our inner peace, and when we make ourselves available to the higher beings by clearing a space in the busy chatter of our lives, who knows what uplifting experience may be made available to us.

Figure 1: <u>Preparation for incarnation</u>

A cloud of living light wraps around what at this stage is my tenuous abstract form; the cloud weaves a light body for me around core memories and feelings.

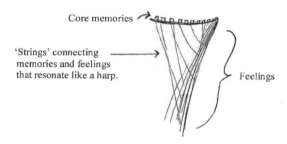

Core memories

'Strings' connecting memories and feelings that resonate like a harp.

Feelings

Figure 2: <u>Our God-Selves, or True Selves</u>

Our God-selves (I've referred to mine earlier as "the largeness of my being") are so powerful they can ray out multiple parallel lives, as well as being the source of our past and future incarnations.

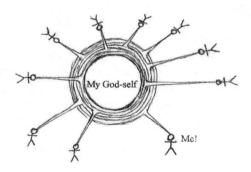

My God-self

Me!

Figure 3: <u>Source</u>

Source, surrounded by droplets of its being that are our personal God-selves. We are like cells in Source's body—we, that is our true selves, are magnificent, and constantly developing as the fruits of Creation are harvested.

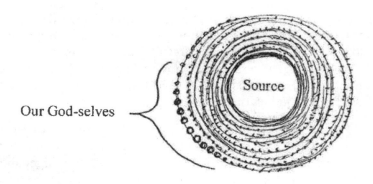

Our God-selves

Chapter 4
Learning Regression Therapy

I treasured every session when I worked with Francesca.

I went deeper and further than I had ever done on my own. Regression is like climbing into a time machine and going on an adventure to find long-lost parts of your self. As a result I came to understand myself much better. I began to recognize how strands of my past selves were woven into my present personality, and I benefited from remembering the lessons they had learned.

When Francesca took me journeying into my other lives I was first made comfortable on a therapy (massage) table and cosseted with blankets and pillows. Warmth and comfort helped me forget about my body and made it easier to relax and feel safe.

As with all inner work I closed my eyes and became still.

A guided relaxation helped me to leave behind the beta level of consciousness that we use in everyday life, where we need its task-oriented concentration, and I began to slip into the more relaxed alpha state of meditation and daydreams. Then it was easy to picture myself in a beautiful place in nature where I could meet with my guardian angel and go on a journey that would take me into the past. **The inner journey always started the same way, but where it went depended on what we were doing.**

***

(1) For *Pre-Creation Soul Therapy* I visualized going to the galaxies and stars, sliding back in time until I became one with Source, *before* Creation. Then I would come forward in time until the part of me that journeys was above my physical body and was easily able to see blockages held in the etheric energy fields of my body.

Blockages can look like gray fog or black dense clouds, and they would be released to the archangels by the power of my will and focused visualization. Francesca used Native American medicine rattles to assist with this, and the powerful scouring sounds of the rattles, combined with vocalized sacred sounds from shamanic traditions literally broke up the ancient stuck energy—because *sound is very powerful when you're in an altered state of consciousness.* The healing was completed when I visualized rebalancing my body with color frequencies of divine energy and transfusions of light.

***

(2) *Regression* meant going back through time, down the centuries, perhaps floating down the millennia to the life I needed to see. The life would be explored and understood, but there was little scope for the deeper healing that sometimes a life cries out for. Well, that was until Dr. Rossetti put the two together!

***

(3) The resulting fusion of soul therapy and regression was termed *Psycho-Regression.* This way of working offers an array of tools for healing the tangles of karma that past lives can throw up. And in this work instead of going back through time you simply scan your body to find where the memories are held.[15]

15 Dr. Rossetti writes about her work in *Psycho-Regression: A New System for Healing & Personal Growth*, published by Piatkus.

People usually do regression to find the root of a problem that will not yield to ordinary means, but you can choose what you look for, and I've found that looking at happy lives can be really helpful. It is like rebooting your psyche. For example, someone was having difficulty getting into a relationship, and when we looked into the problem it was like trying to drain a deep well of loneliness. We found life after life of isolation—he'd been blind, deaf, a slave, etc., etc., but it was only when we looked at a life where he'd been happy, **and he'd been able to see himself enjoying a fulfilling relationship**, that things changed.

I will add that this is never work to be done in a crisis, the client needs to be on an even keel to be able to integrate the experience and deal with whatever they may see in the session. Mum was rarely on an even keel, and for her, spiritual healing would have been more appropriate, certainly to begin with.

Atasha Fyfe, whose book *Magic Past Lives* is published by Hay House, has also found that looking at happy past lives can be most therapeutic. (And it's amazing how often our monastic lives show up as happy! This took me by surprise when it started happening.)

Now while you are engaged in the process of past life recall, it always feels like the most natural thing in the world. Your consciousness feels like it is operating normally, but it is on three simultaneous levels. "Present you" is observing what is going on and can evaluate, make connections, and experience spontaneous realizations as the words tumble out of "old you" in response to the therapist's questions. There is a sense of an over-self, too, a soul level of your being that is enfolding everything, that is aware of both "present you" and "old you." And from this soul level comes the extraordinary information that can be accessed during a session. Soul-you has direct knowing of many things beyond the limits of present you, trapped as we are in time and in the three dimensions in which we live and die.

While exploring the past life story, like a videotape you can fast-forward or rewind the life until you have what you're looking for. If anything unpleasant comes up you can view it like a play or a film without feeling any pain.

Reviewing a life from the vantage point of having just completed it is always valuable, but some lives really benefit from the new perspective we can bring as we look at it afresh, after death. For example, in one of my Native American lives I died feeling a failure.

I had been killed by a bear on the night of a howling wind. It rampaged out of the forest and attacked my family's tipi. It was utterly crazed. In the darkness and the madness of the wind all I could find to fend it off were a couple of tipi poles. I wasn't feeling brave but there was no time to dwell in fear. After a struggle I wedged the tip of one pole down its throat and was able to keep it occupied long enough with the other for my wife to carry our children to safety up a nearby cliff.

The bear crushed my hips and broke my back, but as I looked back on the situation in the therapy session I realized I had done all that was humanly possible. I had bought enough time to save my family, and although I was no longer there to defend them and provide for them, I could see that my brother was going to do that for me. And at last I was able to release the feelings of failure I had carried. I could see my tribe had honored my body and given me what I called "a good death," and that was something which was very important to "old me" and good to see.

The just-after-death point yields the answers to many questions that bring enlightenment and understanding. We are free of the body, and it's as if we float in a sea of knowledge, as if we are no longer so separate from everything. There are no secrets here if you look. As the therapist asks questions the answers are hooked out of the sea of knowledge and float into your mind.[16] But with Psycho-Regression you can go a lot further than intellectually understanding the parallels with your present life because what follows next is the healing and releasing of karma—beginning with *negative emotions* and *negative beliefs* (like about being a failure), *curses, vows*[17] and all sorts of *directed ill-will*, including forms of black magic abuse that may still be lodged within our energy fields. In extreme cases there may be entities, dark angels, or angels of death we're still trailing with us that need to go, even ancient pacts with the devil—it all depends on the life that came up. The etheric counterpart to a sword that killed us can still be wedged in our guts, as can poison or Nazi death camp gas in the lungs. Such things can be the cause of unexplained pains in the body.

Past life injuries can be healed, which is of benefit to weak areas in the present body where the etheric blueprint may have been repeatedly damaged in previous lifetimes.

Unfinished business can be completed.

Forgiveness can make the heart lighter.

Power animals can be connected to—we may have lost our connection with them, and lacking their gifts, the life went wrong.[18] They are our

16 Questions such as whether any of the people in the past life are with you in your present life. Remember, this is for you to know, not to tell the other person. Truthfully you could only say, "Somebody who felt like you did this ..." But as our emotional body expects a repeat, this resemblance will be what's coloring your response to the person in your present life—e.g., why you don't trust them, or why you look to them for a love they can not give. It really might have been them, but I can't stress enough how responsibly you have to handle this.

17 For example, religious vows of poverty, or even the "I will wait for you forever" type, which as well as ruining the original life if the lover in question failed to return, would cause commitment issues in later lives, niggling away in the subconscious undermining new relationships; nobody else would ever feel quite right. Curses fall into many categories and are represented by symbols and words. The spoken word has much more power than you might think when coupled with an emotional charge. (And after my experience with symbols in chapter 3, I realize symbols describe energy – symbols neatly summarize the energy of a curse (or other things). The way to release them is described at the top of page 39.) So to be clear, I don't use symbols in my healing work, but I do help people to release theirs, thus setting themselves free of their influence.

18 Power animals are an important aspect of Native American spirituality, and they offer a way to communicate with Great Spirit and the natural world.

allies in the inner world, and each one offers us a special quality of wisdom that we can draw on.[19]

Soul Retrieval at the end of the session helps us to reclaim and integrate lost fragments of our soul and spirit. Such loss is not the rare event you might think. In our many lifetimes we have often been caught up in traumatic situations and quite literally "fallen apart." Grief or the shock and emotional charge of our reaction to an event (for one past life client it was seeing his family burning to death in a house fire as he looked on, helplessly) can be enough to cause fragments to shatter and stick at that point in space and time. So powerful is "the largeness of our being" that we can still function and go on reincarnating again and again, but eventually we may feel something is missing.[20]

We may have **given away our power** to a master, a temple, or a controlling husband, but no matter what, it too can be retrieved, cleansed, and reintegrated.

And after all the healing of karma I'd consider whether to explore *a new future for the life*. As I began working with people it became apparent that in certain lives there was a pivotal point, perhaps a decision, after which everything went wrong. So having seen where your life choices brought you, and having sorted out the ensuing karma, you are entitled to explore other options and open up a new time line for yourself—although it's more a case of accessing a parallel time line that is already in existence.

***

The work carries great responsibility, and that's why I like working with angels and why I ask for God's help, guidance, and protection at the start of every session. It is not my place to trespass where angels fear to tread, but we certainly do **not** have to remain prisoners of our

---

19 If you would like to work with power animals, but don't want to meet them in meditation or undergo a therapy session, then I recommend using *The Medicine Cards* by Jamie Sams and David Carson published by Bear & Company. The cards are easy to use and great fun. You can just shuffle the pack and pick one to give you the advice you need at any particular time. The message from each animal is contained in the book accompanying the pack, and it's quite spooky how relevant the advice can be.

20 To go into this topic in more depth I recommend Sandra Ingerman's book *Soul Retrieval: Mending the Fragmented Self*. But I counsel that the fragments need cleansing before they're integrated; otherwise, the emotions that caused the split can take days to clear. I do this with sound and the angels' help, but there are ways to visualize it happening.

past. If we choose to understand and learn the lessons the past offers us, we can also heal and let it go… which is why when people ask me, "What if I've been bad?" I say it's not a problem.

After all, it wasn't "present you" who was involved, but "present you" can put matters right, tidy up the karma, and receive a *powerful absolution* from higher powers during the session that will set your soul free. Much better to release the energies from that life than to continue trailing them with you throughout time; they will go on affecting you even if you do nothing, because guilt attracts punishment and bad karma generates bad luck. And we've all been "bad" at one time or another, or if we haven't we will be, because it's part and parcel of the lessons of life, part of the fruits of Creation that we gather as our gift to the Creator.

I'd like to think the techniques Dr. Rossetti evolved with the help of Native American shamans might, in the future, cross-fertilize with other valuable systems of regression to create a powerful worldwide tool for healing. That's my dream—passing the work on, seeing it evolve—and of course we never finish learning.

One weekend while I was at Francesca's home I came across the book *Life between Life* by Dr. Joel L. Whitton and Joe Fisher. It was about people's experiences in what Tibetans call the Bardo. This Tibetan word describes a place, or more accurately the dimensions that we go to between our lives. The accounts were interesting, and they made me want to know more about the stage prior to birth. I wanted to deepen my understanding of the planning that goes on before an incarnation, because sometimes we need answers that can only be found there. But although I really wanted to visit the Bardo I couldn't get Francesca interested in exploring this.

And so it was that one day when I was leafing through *Kindred Spirit* magazine at home I came across my next teacher. The articles in the magazine were interesting, but it's the advertisements I found most intriguing.

Lo and behold, there was an ad offering training in spirit rescue, healing the subtle bodies after surgery, entity release, and **accessing the Bardo**, all with the help of inner guides. The teacher's name was Diane Park.

I had to know more.

Chapter 5
Inner Guides

Diane Park was an Australian who had come to England. Her healing background was in rebirthing, where the breath is an important tool to trigger experience. The people she trained belonged to her Association of Past Life Healers. Like Francesca, she was a woman of great knowledge and experience, but in place of visualization and sound, Diane used visualization and breathing techniques to release unwanted karmic energies. And instead of angels she called upon inner guides to help in her work. She had devised a simple process to enter the inner realms—a script that could just be read out—and to access a past life she favored the device of visualizing descending down steps and entering a hallway with doors.

Each door represented a different life.

You would be drawn to the door you needed to pass through, and you would be questioned on its appearance—which often turned out to have a symbolic significance in relation to the life story that was about to unfold, a life about which you knew absolutely nothing, yet, consciously. Symbols and pictures are the language of the subconscious, and it is always eager to communicate with us.

Having found the door, you visualized opening it—and stepped through into another time, another life. And then the questioning would start to establish who you were and the circumstances of the life you had entered, just as with Francesca's way of working.

Now, angels have great power to help us heal and release, but inner guides understand what it is like to be in a body. They would always be able to give advice. It was like working with a consultant, and particularly useful for looking at the prebirth planning stages when the soul prepares to incarnate. You may have had other options and it can be instructive to look at them, and understand why you chose your present life, picked your parents, and the nature of your mission. As you will remember, when I was considering coming into this life at the beginning of chapter 1, I had guides with me, and help from higher beings like angels.[21]

I like to draw on the services of both for my own work.

It depends on the needs of the client, and there is a fair bit of flexibility in what can be done. For example, after looking at a past life you can meet up with a guide and do some extra work before the session ends— perhaps visit the Bardo to check on your life plan, or have a guide bring your recently departed loved one to meet with you for a conversation.

I had been interested in guides ever since 1985 when a good friend gave me Edwin C. Steinbrecher's *The Inner Guide Meditation: A Transformational Journey to Enlightenment and Awareness* published by Aquarian Press. The instructions in the book made it easy for me to meet my main guide, Francis, and told me how to work with him.

The book explained how inner guides and spirit guides are the same thing. They are usually people who have known you in a previous lifetime who are in spirit awaiting their next incarnation. The love they have for you makes them want to help you. They know how hard it can be to gather spiritual riches on the Earth plane.[22]

Volunteering to work as a guide is one of the few ways to work off karma when you are not in a body, and it is the discomfort of our karmic load that pulls us from the bliss of the world of spirit back into the world of form time and again. We can't rest for long in the realms of light burdened with the irritation of our own darkness. It feels very uncomfortable, like having a stone in your shoe, and as this feeling grows we long to shake off the karmic irritation and fill ourselves with more love and bliss. In short, we come to long for another life as it is the best way to shed karma and gather love.

---

21 The conversations were telepathic, but they did take place. You are involved in the choice and actually have to agree with the final decision, although the spiritual perspective is very different from what you might expect. I didn't like the wounds I'd set up once I got down here!

22 Francis had been my abbot in eleventh-century England. I'd taken refuge from the brutality that followed the Norman Conquest in 1066, and become a monk. I particularly enjoyed making illuminated manuscripts, singing and growing the vegetables we ate. It was a simple but satisfying life. Francis will have had other lives after that, but he appears to me in a way I can recognize him, looking like he used to look when we were together. Bless him.

It is, if only we can remember why we came!

Our hearts never forget, but our minds do to spare us confusion. It would be even harder to resist the temptation to return to the bliss when confronted by the karmic challenges that brought us, and can you imagine how maddening and disorientating it would be for a child to be swamped with memories of multitudes of past life personalities? Our memories slip safely into our subconscious, and even from there they try to protect us through our fears and phobias, our attractions and repulsions.

Hearts constantly remind us why we're here. They open when we are loving, and we feel a nice warm glow inside, but when we are mean they close and shrink and we feel empty. Empty never feels good. We may try to fill the emptiness with food or use alcohol as a temporary anesthetic, and the search to dull the pain can lead on to destructive behavior although it was meant to guide us back to being loving.

All actions in life create karma, good or bad. The universal Law of Karma is like the Law of Gravity: the falling apple is always drawn to the ground while karma is returned to the soul who made it, so that the soul can experience what it has set in motion. It is the simple mechanism by which we learn and grow spiritually.

The karma of our good and loving actions is experienced as good fortune, but bad karma feels as if we are being punished by fate in a cruel and random world. Some strands of our karma may take several lifetimes to work out, but work out they will, because we live in a universe that is ultimately just. As Jesus said in the Bible,[23] Galations

---

23 The Holy Bible, rev. ed. (Cambridge: Cambridge University Press, 1924); my granddad's Bible. As you know, Granddad died when I was six months old, and I should have liked to have met him. But while learning about spirit rescue with Diane Park, I did meet him in the inner world— when to my surprise a spirit rescue guide took me to the churchyard where Grandma, his wife, is buried with him in the family grave. Apparently, Grandma had spent the years after death flitting between the graveyard and the hospital where she died. *She'd missed the light that takes us up into the spiritual world*—**because she was waiting for the vicar to take her to heaven.** This would have been ridiculous if it wasn't so sad. She'd been an ardent churchgoer for years, and had placed more faith in the vicar than I ever imagined. But with the help of the specialist guide things were explained to her, and Granddad came down with the light and took her up into it. I liked what I sensed about my granddad very much. I hadn't expected to get something so personal out of the rescue session, it's usually more of a service you render to the departed of the world, without having actually known the people in life.

6:7:

> *Be not deceived; God is not mocked:* **whatsoever a man soweth, that shall he also reap.**

Jesus's words about reincarnation have been edited by time and the hands of men, but there still remains a reference in the book of St. John (8:56–58), when Jesus says to the Pharisees:

> 56 *Your father Abraham rejoiced to see my day; and he saw it, and was glad.*

> 57 The Jews therefore said unto him, Thou art not yet fifty years old, and hast thou seen Abraham?

> 58 Jesus said unto them, *Verily, verily I say unto you,* **Before Abraham was, I am.**

I've come across people who say, "Past lives are against Jesus," but there is nothing to suggest this in the Bible; and the lost teachings of reincarnation are to be found in the pages of this book.

In fact, looking at the journey of your soul can only increase your awe and respect for God.

Unlocking the secrets of past lives has become my passion. Past life work answers the big existential questions of life. It makes it easy to see why you are here, it unravels the mystery of death and shows you that love has the power to transcend space and time. It's always good to understand more about yourself, and it is a sure way to do that. The more we know ourselves the more we can love and accept ourselves, and we're all working on that one! After all, you can't love a stranger.

This is the time in the world where we release the past, having gratefully received its lessons, so we can step boldly into the new dawn. It's a

---

Spirit rescue is an interesting topic. There's always something holding a ghost, tying it to the world—but with a specialist guide for advice this can be understood and renegotiated. The spirit has lost logic and is trapped in a loop, like the suicide who jumped off of a cliff and endlessly fell and returned to the top of the cliff and jumped again. This loop has to be broken before they can move on. The spirit needs to be talked to by someone in our level of reality so that the guides can intercede. In the case mentioned here, a young woman had lost the love of her life, watched him sail off to America leaving her bereft on the cliffs of Ireland. It was a bit of a struggle, but in the end we got her to visit an animal she loved. Once she was away from the cliff edge the loop was broken and she was successfully helped.

time for facing up to karma because we can't carry it through into the Age of Aquarius. Planetary energies are changing, and there's a lot of karma that will have to be worked out in the world in a very short time. That's why we are experiencing a rough ride at present: it's the massive karmic return clearing the decks so we can sail into the golden future. So why not do it a quicker, gentler way—**in the inner world**? We can wait for the millstones of fate to refine us, or we can choose to use our God-given intelligence and understand karma's lessons for ourselves.

The ideal situation for doing past lives is working with a therapist you trust, but if time and budget don't allow for that, it's amazing how much you can achieve on your own. Denise Linn's book *Past Lives, Present Miracles: How to Use Reincarnation for Personal Growth* is an excellent guide for do-it-yourself experiences that are effective.

My work has brought me inner peace, and it prepared me for what was coming my way in 1992. The Bible's words, "And God created man in his own image... male and female created he them," were about to take on a whole new meaning (Genesis 1:27), and I was to see what puts the "solar"[24] into solar plexus. But you never know what your next mystical experience is going to teach you—as I was about to find out...

---

24 Meaning "of the sun."

Chapter 6

Enlightenment, Soul Mates, and Seeing the Light Within

Just to put this experience in the context of my life I need to give you a quick summary so far—because we've been following the thread of healing, but there had been other things going on which I've just hinted at. It's time to flesh them out. So: in the late 1960s I'd been a student. In September 1971 I'd become an art teacher, and in 1974 I got married.

We'd known each other since I was a student, and I thought I knew my husband well. We'd lived together for a couple of years before we took the plunge, but he changed after we got married. Another side of him surfaced. It was a short and unhappy marriage that took me to live in Germany and lasted only eighteen months before we separated. (My mother died during this time.) My husband was English, but he was working on the Meteosat project at the European Space Agency in Darmstadt. This is the project that monitors our weather by satellite and provides weather pictures for TV news in the UK and Europe.

He had an affair and told me to return to England.

I did, but I wanted more than to return to our old house full of memories.

A friend was moving to Cornwall to study art. So I sold up and bought a house there. Cornwall is the southernmost tip of England; it's like an arm that stretches out toward the Atlantic Ocean. It has a romantic history because over the centuries smugglers used the sea caves and hidden coves to bring ashore brandy, perfume, lace, and wines from France to escape paying taxes. There's many a romantic novel set in Cornwall, and today because it is pretty, it is popular with tourists. The streets are lined with picturesque old buildings, it has beautiful beaches, and it looks idyllic. But although I enjoyed this holiday episode in my life, Cornwall never felt like home. I filled a folio with drawings and paintings and gave a lecture on Gaudi at the art school in Falmouth, where I lived. But as I walked along the streets the granite curbstones told me I was a stranger. The hard, volcanic granite was not the rock of home. I felt as though I was running away. I was forced to take stock of my life because the certainty of youth had gone. I'd turned thirty, and I was lost in a wilderness, drifting without purpose. I came across the Carlos Castaneda books, took yoga classes, and continued to visit the Mind Body Spirit festivals, but the pain of being off my true path was like having barbed wire inside me, and it pushed me to take action.

I lived in Cornwall for only eighteen months.

Manchester was where I'd been happiest, so I returned.[25] I bought a lovely house and a kiln and rebuilt my life there at the end of the 1970s. The house was big enough to set up a little pottery studio. It had a generous garden, charming colored glass in the old windows, spacious rooms, and a big dry cellar. It was perfect! I loved it. But things were to go wrong again… when I got sucked into someone else's dream. I foolishly mortgaged my home for a business venture to help a new partner, someone I'd met on my return to Manchester. The enticement was that the restaurant would provide a small income for me as I got the pottery off the ground. But that's not how it worked out.

It was a wholefood restaurant in the city center that was far too idealistic in concept, and though there was no shortage of customers, as a financial venture *Wild Oats* was not a success. The business development loan that had financed it was secured against my house, and that was possibly the stupidest thing I've ever done. Because although I left the restaurant in 1983, my ex-partner sold it for a huge loss in 1984, then declared himself bankrupt—so the entire loan fell to me to repay. For several years I thought I would lose my home. It was a very worrying time. I'd certainly taken another wrong turn in the maze of life.

So you can see that when I was thirty-five in 1983 I was precipitated into a midlife crisis.

I had to reassess everything, because nothing was working out.

I had to make changes.

I had to leave the restaurant.

---

25   Writing this I looked on Google and found that Manchester, like Frodsham, is built on sandstone; there's something about sandstone and me.

I had a dream whose message was so clear it needed no decoding. In the dream I was climbing out of a deep hole in the ground, and my partner was behind me trying to pull me back. I kicked out at him, to shake him off, and shouted at him in fury. I awoke knowing it was over and that he was holding me back. There was an overwhelming feeling of having to escape. On paper I was still trapped in my marriage because I'd never got round to divorcing my husband—I'd felt too traumatized to consider this before because it kept me safe from having to make any decisions about settling down again. But now I sorted out the divorce.

I was ready to move on, perhaps even get remarried, should I find the right person.

I changed my name by deed poll and took my mother's surname. I didn't want to go back to my maiden name—I wasn't that person anymore, but there was no way I was keeping my ex's surname any longer. And while I was about it I changed the spelling of Pauline to Paulinne[26] to bring my new name into numerical harmony with my birth date. All due to the influence of books and numerology! But it did stop me from feeling like a victim of life. The most important thing came next.

As a child I used to attend Sunday school at the church in Frodsham. One Sunday we had been visited by missionaries talking about their work in Africa. They said they had been *called by God* to do this work. That really scared me, young as I was, and I never forgot it. I didn't want to be "called," I didn't want to have to obey God and lose my freedom to live life as I chose, and right then and there I'd said, "God, I'm not listening." But now I could see how I had made a mess of things, my disastrous first marriage had been followed by the disastrous business venture where I nearly lost everything including my home, and there actually came a moment when I said to God: "I *am* listening now. If there is something I've come to do, let's start."

That's when I went on to explore healing and past lives, found my true purpose in life—and eventually found happiness with a second husband. All I'd given up was the freedom to make myself miserable! Telling God I was willing was like switching on the computer program for "my becoming," taking me on a journey to become more of myself, as I unfolded into my gifts while being borne along on the flow of life. **Thinking of God as an enemy had been the problem.**

***

---

26 Said Pau-lynne (but both ways are good).

And how exactly did I meet my lovely second husband? I put an advertisement in the personal column of Manchester's *City Life* magazine. I felt cheeky telling the universe that I was not satisfied with the cards I had been dealt in life, but I just knew I had to make a gesture. Shake the dice a bit harder. Do *something*. I only paid for one insertion of the ad, but walking back from the post box I already felt better.

I had a few replies, people sent letters, and then came a postcard with a photo attached. It was from a "Ye Min." Ye is a Burmese name (said Yay here, but in Burma it would be Yeah). But although Ye had been born in Burma, his parents actually lived in England, and apart from the first few months of his life he'd been brought up in London. It was typical of Ye's liking for brevity to send a postcard. His poems are always pared to the bone.

Ye had lived in England all his life, and sounded totally English when we spoke on the phone; he had such a lovely voice that when I heard it I sort of knew. He now lived nearby, in Warrington. We arranged to meet at the Cornerhouse art gallery in Manchester for coffee—and when our eyes met as he came toward me in the street I knew we had a connection through space and time. I really felt it.

Weeks later I tidied his postcard away and noticed the box number he'd replied to. It wasn't the one I'd paid for. It turned out the magazine had run my ad several times, and he'd replied through one of the other box numbers. When I examined the number he'd answered it was 10702. My birthday is the 10th and I've always regarded 7 as God's number, a special sacred number, and Ye's birthday is the 2nd. What was the chance of that? I thought it was spooky, like God saying you can't cheat destiny. So I didn't feel cheeky anymore. It felt like we were destined to meet (and I found out we knew two people in common).[27]

Ye taught handicapped children in a special needs school, and he was interested in dramatherapy. We were both teachers and both interested in therapies of different kinds. He swept me off my feet, and the summer we met was a very happy time. It was 1988. I was forty.

We married on Valentine's Day in 1989.

I was totally smitten.

---

27 Remember the beginning of chapter 1? I wonder if our association of angels playing harps in heaven, coupled with the sacredness attributed to the number 7, has anything to do with our subliminal memories of the prebirth state. (See Figure 1 on page 36.)

We are soul mates and we've been together many times, in many lives, and even on other worlds. And although it didn't seem likely at the time, Ye would eventually come to train as a past life therapist himself.

***

Now when I met Ye he had a young son, Jo, from an earlier marriage. He and Jo had both been in the photo he'd sent, so I'd known about him from the start. Jo's birth mother had died years before I met him, and he was pleased to have a new mum. Jo and I liked each other and really got on. He was a sweet little nine-year-old boy who had always wanted brothers and sisters—and before the end of 1991 we'd given him two sisters, Rose and Clio Isadora. I didn't manage to give him any brothers, because I had my hands completely full with his sisters!

The lovely house I'd bought in South Manchester made a great family home, and so Ye sold his house in Warrington and took over the loan repayments.

But having children is exhausting, especially later in life.

I never had enough sleep—and there was no more keeping a dream journal! Oh, the luxury of all the time you have to yourself when you live on your own. But it was a very happy time when the children were little.

To combat the exhaustion I tried homeopathy, Chinese herbs, and then I consulted Kitty Campion. Kitty was a well-known herbalist, and one of my friends was studying with her. I diligently took Kitty's herbs, did a fast, and undertook a lemon juice and olive oil liver flush, which I have to confess was grim. But it was at Kitty's suggestion that I went to the Cortijo Romero center in Spain in 1992—which turned out to be one of the best things I ever did in all my life.

Dr. Richard Shulze was over from the United States, and he had joined forces with Kitty to run some courses there. All the participants were on a healing journey for one reason or another.

Our week had begun with a three-day juice fast to cleanse and detox our systems. On the evening of the third day we brought the blankets off our beds into the meeting room, and after warm-up exercises we lay on the floor and made ourselves comfortable. The lights were dimmed and candles flickered. Gently rising waves of Sufi trance music lapped around us. I relaxed with no idea of what was in store for me. (And when we talked about it the next day we found everyone had had a different experience.)[28]

We were directed and encouraged to breathe continuously without pausing between our breaths. I shut my eyes and did this connected breathing. I soon began to feel different. My brain felt as if it was being flooded with oxygen. My hands felt strange, as though I had rounded sensitive pads extending from the ends of my fingers—and my left hand felt like it was wearing a ring and bracelet, where no such things existed. So real did they feel that I checked with my right hand, but my fingers passed through the energy field where they were, and found nothing that was tangible in these dimensions. Then things got stranger still.

A radiant living sun beamed above me, its surface covered in moving tongues of silver-gray fire. It moved closer and came within me. It became my solar plexus, and it brought with it the realization that I was a part of God, as we all are, every last one of us, and I understood the joke of life. As God I had wanted to learn about sorrow, pain, loss, and death—all things that were not a part of Me, new things that I wanted to explore which Creation had made possible—and I had set up life after life for this purpose. I would enter each life with enthusiasm but then try to avoid the lessons when they came! I would always try to duck them! But there's no escaping yourself, and it was just so hilarious that I laughed out loud again and again. It was the classic "joke of life." It was literally "enlightenment" because I had seen the light of God within me and the light had shown me this.[29]

Once before, and only once, during a profound spiritual healing, when my thoughts had gone to God I'd glimpsed the same sun. The dimensions of the world had parted as God's light penetrated matter and rayed down around the healee and me, and when we had finished we both knew something extraordinary had occurred.

But now the joke of life had me wracked with laughter. Loud crazy laughs welled up from the depths of my being and rolled around the ceiling.

---

28   The music is available on a CD called *el-Hadra* (*the Mystic Dance*), by Klaus Wiese. I loved it so much I had to buy it.

29   Calls to mind Moses's experience with the burning bush: the fire that does not consume, coupled with the voice of God.

I was laughing and looking up at the rafters when I caught sight of a hooded figure approaching. It drew nearer. From beneath the dark hood a white skull face peered down at me. Laughter froze in my chest. This was Death. The Grim Reaper had come for me.

But then I remembered something. Grasping at the memory I knew this wasn't the first time I'd met him. He had come to my rescue before. Times beyond the counting he had taken me out of impossible situations, and I'd been so pleased to see him then, that now I rose out of my body to greet my old friend, and we danced a mad, joyful jig. We danced right out of the room and into the gardens until we were over the swimming pool, and on and on we danced, over the waters shimmering in moonlight.

Then as quickly as he had come, Death was gone. I was aware of being back in my body, lying on the floor, in the room.

Now that I'd lost all fear of death multitudes of fear entities began shooting out of me. My energy field was no longer compatible with theirs and they could not stay. I had to twist from side to side and stretch from my waist to create enough room for their escape, and as I curved my body and moved about I exclaimed, "Oh shit!" because of the extreme nature of the feeling and the overwhelming speed with which they were being released from my guts. I felt like I was a champagne bottle that had been shaken and uncorked and the fizz was exploding out of me.

The word "shit" triggered another realization: it is "the ultimate product of the divine vehicle." "Divine vehicle" meaning our body, as it is the vehicle carrying our divine spirit through life. To live and stay in body we have to fuel it by eating. We take into ourselves the substances the Creator has provided, and our body transforms this food into the ultimate product of the digestive process, our feces. Looking at it this way imbues it with a spiritual quality, and I realized we should be enriching our lands and blessing the planet with this wonderful manure, instead of flushing it away, treating it as a nuisance…

Then I remembered the entities. They were still in the pool where I'd tossed them as a temporary containment, but now I felt responsible for them. Unwittingly I had created them out of the energy of my thoughts and emotions over many lifetimes, and I couldn't just leave them lying around waiting to attach themselves to other people and increase their burden of fears. So I did what I would in any past life situation, I asked the archangels to take them to wherever they needed to be to complete their evolution. They were as much a part of the universe as anything else, and like all such entities they needed help to spiritualize their energy and move up the spiral of being.

After the archangels took them I felt calmer and more peaceful.

I mentioned earlier that I was in Spain that week because of my perpetual exhaustion. I had had my children late in life and I loved them dearly, but looking after young children is very demanding and there had been many nights of broken sleep. In the depth of my tiredness I would ache for "home," a world where the sky was pink and things were so much easier. Now I began to glimpse some of my lives on other worlds, and I realized that things were not easier or even better there, just different. The lessons may change, but the lessons of life definitely do not stop.

The glorious pink light of some sunsets—when substantial clouds are underlit by orange-pink light and the whole sky glows—had made me yearn for this other world, but afterward I felt reconciled to dear old Earth and grateful to be here. When I thought of my children I felt gratitude again, this time to my husband, Ye, for making it possible for me to be in Spain having this experience, and for giving me the intense pain of childbirth, twice! This was obviously not the way I had previously viewed it, but now I was comprehending something much deeper about the nature of pain: it is a paradox. It is bad, but it is good. It is a powerful spiritual purge, and not a drop ever goes to waste.

The final insight was that my exhaustion was caused by my resistance to life. The way I was living was like driving a car with the hand brake on. I was bracing myself to meet life as a series of demands when I should flow with it as an adventure. I had been wearing myself out with this attitude.

At the end of the week I returned to my family in Manchester, but as a reminder of my experience I put four little white stones on the shelf below the mirror in our hall. I love stones and crystals and often pick up small ones as souvenirs from places, and these were from the trip. Every time I came or went I passed the stones and seeing them reminded me that the illusion of matter hides a greater reality. Flying back from Spain had taken us high above the clouds where the sunshine was beautiful. On rainy days in Manchester I would remember that above the clouds the sun was still shining, and it cheered me up. Just because we can't see it does not mean it's not there. And that's how it is with God.

* * *

Soul Mates

We all belong to a soul group; it's our very own special cosmic family.

We don't have just one soul mate connection, but potentially many—and they may be our parents or children, or friends, just as easily as they could be our partner. It's like the soul group is taking the same exams in life and is at the same point of initiation in spiritual evolution. I believe we have a twin flame too—a very special being who shares our spirit energy, who is literally part of us. But these relationships can be very fraught and intensely powerful and not necessarily happy. It is said we can acquire awesome bad karma with a twin flame and be kept apart for many lifetimes. Soul mates understand each other and are much more easy-going.

"Twin flame" comes from the fact that our spirit body is composed of divine fire—silvery, higher dimensional, living fire—it's our **God body/causal body/I Am Presence/divine monad/God-self**—from which we ray down enough of our spirit essence to go into a physical body and give rise to another personality, another adventure into matter, another lifetime or existence somewhere. And it was this living-light-of-God-fire that I'd just seen in my experience at Cortijo Romero.

Chapter 7
Connecting with the Crystal Skulls

Every year that passed got easier with the children, and by 1994 I had the time and energy to teach a small group of students who were interested in past lives. One Sunday a month we had a day where I demonstrated and then they practiced. It gave me the discipline to write the process down, and we compiled a big file of notes on all the aspects of regression I'd learned from Diane and Francesca. They were lovely people and one of them, Annie, could see auras. What an amazing gift that must be. I had a dream once where I could see them, but I was very disappointed when I woke up and still found that I couldn't!

I was able to do a lot of past life sessions with my students, and some very valuable research. This was when I founded The Association of Past Life and Soul Therapists, and when Ye began training in the work.

But the next big thing that happened was in 1996.

Ye and I saw an intriguing documentary about the crystal skulls on BBC television.

Well, I love crystals, and I'd heard about the skulls; by chance I'd even seen the British Museum's skull when it was on display in the Museum of Mankind in London. But it was only when I watched the program that I began to have any understanding of the skulls' significance. The program made a big impression on me, and it really sparked my interest. Then as luck would have it we met the film's makers.

Chris Morton and Ceri Louise Thomas were living in Manchester while finishing work on their book, *The Mystery of the Crystal Skulls*. We became friends, and when the book came out Chris and Ceri gave us a copy. As I held it I knew it was something very special, but I didn't know why it gave me a feeling no book ever had before. This book was intriguing and inspiring, but it was so much more than that.

It told of Native American legends about the skulls, legends that were held by the Mayan and Aztec descendants in Central America, the Pueblo and Navajo Indians of the southwestern United States, right up to the Cherokee and Seneca Indians in the northeast of the USA.

The legends spoke of thirteen ancient crystal skulls, the size of human skulls, that held information on our origins, purpose, and destiny—and answers to the greatest mysteries of life and the universe—and they foretold a time when this information would be vital to the very survival of the human race; that though the skulls have been scattered and hidden, one day they will be reunited so their collective wisdom can save us from disaster.

Chris and Ceri had thought this just a colorful story until they learned that a skull had been found in some ancient Mayan ruins, and since then other skulls had come to light... All were of mysterious origin and surrounded by tales of paranormal activity and psychic or healing powers.

It had set them off on a quest to find the truth—a quest which took them to deserts and tropical rainforests, to scientists and shamans, to the British Museum in London, and to the laboratories of Hewlett-Packard and the cold snows of Canada. At sacred gatherings of native elders they learned of the ancient wisdom of the skulls and heard alarming prophecies for our immediate future. Charged with spreading the important message before it is too late, their book is the story of their remarkable discoveries, and it tells that the skulls' guardians have already begun the *bringing together*... because the time of danger is now!

It was a cracking read and felt very important to me, but it was much more than that. Because although I didn't know it, destiny and fate were making connections, connecting me with the skulls.

I simply had no idea of the strength of my link with them back then. No idea that it had developed over many lifetimes; that I'd been a skull guardian, and engaged with them in other dimensions, even on other worlds; and that this robust contact with them continues to the present day because in a past life I'd undertaken to render them a service—undertaken to tell their story and deliver a message carried in my soul memory for fifteen hundred years. (And you can find it in *Holy Ice*, my second book, which is where the crystal-skull-related treasures properly belong.) In *Holy Ice* I reveal where the legend originated, and how it came about.

Because it is indeed true.

And it is indeed important.

***

The other thing about 1996 was that it was a year Ye had no work. Life's crises and challenges sometimes bring us a gift. If Ye had been working we would not have met Chris and Ceri at a daytime dance class; and if my first marriage hadn't broken down I would not have met Ye, had my children, and had a long and happy marriage.

***

Ye's career was to take us north. He soon found employment as a dramatherapist in the North East of England. He was working with children for a charity called Total Learning Challenge. For a while he commuted, living in the seaside town of Whitley Bay during the week, but returning home at the weekend. When it was clear the work was going well, we decided to sell up and move north. In the autumn of 1998 we were house hunting in the North East of England when I heard that some of the crystal skulls and their guardians were visiting the area. It was the year of the Wolf Song 1X World Peace Elders tour, and Mary Thunder and many indigenous elders from around the world had come to Northumberland in time for the September equinox. I could hardly believe it.

There was no question.

I had to go to see them.

During a day of interesting talks they introduced us to the crystal skulls they had with them. Nick Nocerino's skull Sha Na Ra was available for private sittings, so with mounting excitement I put my name down on the list.

Now, the North East has some lovely beaches, and after the polluted air of Manchester we were considering living by the sea. Ye was thinking of a house in Whitley Bay, but I had misgivings. I had an irrational fear of inundations and death by tsunami.

When my turn came to look into the crystal depths of the skull I focused on the burning question of the moment: should we buy a house in Whitley Bay? Would we be safe by the sea? After all that I'd read in Chris and Ceri's book, here I was, face-to-face with an ancient and authentic skull. Would it show me pictures, would it speak to me?

Nothing happened.

I continued holding my question and staring into it, hands gently touching it.

Then I relaxed the focus of my eyes. A clear picture of a peaceful, welcoming sea appeared within the skull, with no sign of the tsunami of my deepest fears. I had been given the answer—the skull had said "yes" with a picture. And although I didn't know it, I'd done this before—but in other lives, lives lived long ago, in a land now hidden beneath the wild ocean's waves, a land some think of as no more than a myth… Atlantis, ancient jewel of the Atlantic.

I still knew nothing about my past life connections with the skulls. However, I was certainly attracted to them… and now they had begun to communicate with me.[30]

We found a pretty seaside home, and at the end of March 1999 we moved in.

We loved living near the golden sands of Whitley Bay. At low tide the sea drew back to expose terraces of sandstone rocks studded with rock pools, and although not the red of my childhood sandstone, they were comforting, and so beautifully sculpted and smoothed by the waves. Every time I saw the sea my heart leapt, and the ever-changing silvers and pearly, gray-blue velvet colors of the North Sea's restless waves entranced me.

Our girls settled down in their new schools and through them I met people. I still love to walk by the sea and stop for coffee in one of the cafés with my friends.

I decorated the house and transformed the garden. I love flowers and I even won a gardening competition. I put my roots down, you could say; and to learn more about medicinal herbs and aromatherapy oils I did a few hours a week in the old Neal's Yard Remedies shop in picturesque Central Arcade in Newcastle-upon-Tyne's city center. Newcastle is

---

30 I was so attracted I'd made a thirteen quartz skulls necklace in honor of the legend, and wore it to the event! I'd strung the skull beads interspersed with river pearls to represent their pearls of wisdom. That's so keen, I should have guessed there was a very strong connection.

close by, and it has some beautiful old buildings. I enjoyed the buzz of the city and I loved helping customers to choose natural remedies for their own healing. And at Christmas the city's lights looked like a carpet of stars as you looked down Grey Street (named after Earl Grey, he of the famous tea!) from the arcade.

Working in the shop and developing our garden were grounding activities for me, and provided a valuable counterbalance to the heady nature of past life work.

I gave talks about my work, did demonstrations, and took clients, and through leaving a past life flyer at Pax, a healing center in Whitley Bay, I was to meet Veronica Fyland. Veronica was a local crystal therapist and gifted hypnotherapist. She was experienced in past life work, was studying sound therapy, and was interested in finding out about the shamanic aspects of my work and the ways I used sound. Veronica has many ways of working, and I found I'd had some misconceptions about hypnotherapy. I came to trust Veronica. We began to exchange sessions in the beautiful room I'd made into a healing sanctuary in my home.

When she worked with me she took me into the inner world, and like Diane Park had done, she would direct me to go down steps and then enter a hallway with doors—one of which was going to take me into the past life I needed to see; it was good to use such a familiar journey, and it made it easy for me to work with Veronica.

She has other ways to work, but this was to help me.

Now since I was a child I'd known I had a book to write. Over the years there were various attempts to start but nothing got very far. I had a lot of interesting past life material by now, but no focus for it, no structure for a book, and after we moved to Whitley Bay I grew more and more frustrated.

I had dreams telling me not to be impatient. In one I was wearing trainers and trying to run with a baby in a pram. The baby was the book, the new project, and racing with it felt inappropriate. A dream's message lies in the feeling you have about the actions in the dream, and this was clear. In another dream I saw a room full of gorgeous butterflies and I knew each one was a book, or ideas for books. But I could neither catch the butterflies nor release them, I couldn't interact with them, I was a frozen observer.

It wasn't until the autumn of 2007 that everything changed. As if the butterflies had landed on me, higher guidance gave me the title and structure for my writing. It literally dropped into my mind, the title more beautiful than I could have devised, complete with clear instructions for the message I was to convey. **I was to reveal secrets lost in time:**

1. **Beginning with lost teachings of Jesus,**

2. **Going on to penetrate the mystery of the crystal skulls,**

3. **Finishing by exploring the future,**

—all to help with the challenge our species is facing now, because we're at a pivotal point in our destiny. It could be heaven or hell on Earth—we choose—but this will help us, because *knowledge is power.*

***

I didn't know what I was going to discover—*Spiritual Gold, Holy Ice, Divine Fire*—that was the title, and you must admit *Divine Fire* has a rather ominous ring to it for a book about the future! The topics linked together because the future and the path of our spiritual evolution are entwined. (At that point I didn't realize it was going to grow so big it would turn into three separate books. It took Nancy Vernon at Ozark Mountain Publishing to wake me up to that, in April 2016, when she kindly returned my original manuscript. I'd naively assumed it was just one book.)

***

The secrets were to be dug out of my own previous lifetimes, so that would mean doing a lot of new regression sessions in the hunt to unearth the material.

I knew I had actually heard Jesus speak, because I'd accessed this in 2002 while preparing a talk entitled "Creating Heaven on Earth," which was given at the Mind, Body, Spirit Northern Festival held at G-Mex, the big exhibition center in Manchester. (After a previous sell-out workshop there on guides and angels, I'd been their celebrity speaker for three years running, even after I left Manchester. Back in the 1970s at the Mind Body Spirit in London I'd felt like a hungry child who was standing in the street looking into a sweet-shop window, but now I was well and truly inside the sweet shop, and more than that, I was sharing out the sweets! Back then I never dreamed I'd have treasure enough to share.)... But another regression would be needed to catch the words of Jesus's teachings because the original tapes from 2002 had gone missing. Everything else would have to be researched from scratch.

Then I had my first stroke of luck.

Veronica offered to do the regressions, and we set off together on a voyage of discovery.

We taped each session and I transcribed the tapes by longhand.

If I needed to fill in extra details afterward I did this through meditation.

My dear friend Hana gave me her laptop, so typing up the chapters was easy. And Isabelle, one of the friends I enjoyed coffee with by the sea, said she'd like that most essential of jobs, to be the "first reader." Isabelle pointed out plenty of gaps I was too close to see. Her questions were invaluable.

Generally the chapters followed a pattern of being introduced by pertinent additional material, then the lives would unfold, and after the life story came comments relevant to the journey of the soul.

I worked on draft after draft. I'm a night owl, and in the quiet hours at the end of the day after family duties had been discharged, I did most of my writing alone with our cats. The house was peaceful then. I could hear myself think. Each autumn after a short summer break I came back to the book with new eyes. It had a life of its own. I had the tantalizing feeling it already existed on the etheric levels, and that I was merely trying to remember it... and as time passed more information came my way and we did ever more regressions.

But it was when the writing was finished that the most amazing stroke of luck occurred.

I met Guy Steven Needler. Guy is a successful author who has many books published by Ozark Mountain Publishing (OMP) in the United States, and he very kindly offered to read my writing and was extremely generous with his advice. In July 2015 he took my manuscript to Ozark when he went to speak at their annual Transformation Conference.

OMP was established by Dolores Cannon, the famous American regressionist who used deep trance to great effect in her quantum healing work. Her many books are full of remarkable material gained that way, and I confess Dolores has been an inspiration to me over the years, and I certainly recommend her books to you. Long ago I was stopped in my tracks by *Keepers of the Garden*. Before her death in 2014 she trained thousands of practitioners worldwide; and there's no doubt that the material she brought forth through her regression techniques has helped nudge our collective consciousness up the evolutionary spiral of understanding. She has made an enormous contribution to the raising of our collective consciousness. I attended many of her talks when she came to England over the years, and at a Past Life Conference in the 1990s I actually asked Dolores if she'd write the foreword to my book. At that stage I was busy with an earlier attempt that fell by the wayside, and this was years before she set up OMP. At the time Element handled her work. She graciously said I should send my book to her via Element when it was finished—this shows both the high esteem in which I held Dolores, and the frustratingly long wait it would be before the book finally crystallized out of the ethers.

Well, it's here at last—and thank you, Dolores, for all that you've done to open our minds.

***

So the stories you're about to read are true.

They are fact, not fiction. They are far memories from some of my other lifetimes that have been recovered through regression—mostly working with Veronica, a hypnotherapist, but also through work influenced by Psycho-Regression, as devised by Dr. Francesca Rossetti. These particular lives have been selected by my higher self because they show what we need to remember at this crucial time, and scattered through the chapters are keys to wake us up. I don't know what the keys are, but I believe what higher guidance has told me, and I do know the next few years are vital. They are going to determine our future for better or for worse.

I'm hoping this book will change the way you view things and perhaps change the way you think about things, because thought is the most powerful tool we have to create the future we want. Thought helps things manifest. It's thought that will bring the evolutionary shift in our consciousness that is vital if we are to survive, if we are to enter a golden age and not slide into the pit of oblivion.

This is a book I had to write.

This is something I promised to do lifetimes ago.

And it *is* truly remarkable how help flowed in to make it happen.

But that was because someone else was keeping their promise...

Remember the promise at the very beginning?

... Jesus?

Chapter 8
Jesus and the Lost Teachings of Reincarnation

This is the most important chapter. It could save your life—because whatever events are being drawn to you by bad karma, you do not have to experience them. There is a way out. Love can set you free. In the alchemical fires of love your karma is transmuted into spiritual gold; karma has to return to the same person but if you are no longer that, because through love you have changed, then the Law of Grace steps in.

This is the truth about love. Love transcends karma.

And Jesus came to tell us about love, so read on!

Finding Nadia

We all find our own right time to come to past lives, and it's not something that should ever be hurried. You will know when you're ready to look at one of your previous lifetimes—you have to want it, *really want it*—and curiosity or need has to be stronger than the understandable fear of doing something new, something that seems a bit scary and different. It took Ye quite a while to get to this place.

He had seen me demonstrate and heard me give talks about my work while we lived in Manchester during the 1990s, but for a long time he wasn't interested in looking at a past life himself. He had been brought up in a Buddhist household in London by Burmese parents, and he was well used to the idea of reincarnation, so it wasn't that he had a problem with the concept. He was a special needs teacher working with handicapped children, and a dramatherapist in his own right by now, so he was no stranger to therapy, but it took a serious falling out with someone close to him before he was ready to get on my therapy couch for the very first time.

He wanted to see if hidden past life dynamics were fueling the difficult situation. (Little did he know he'd enjoy it and end up as a past life therapist!) He got so much out of the session that it was the first of many, and unexpectedly he felt I had been his wife in the earlier incarnation too. Although I already knew we'd been together many times before, I was curious. I checked it out, and when I was regressed by one of my Manchester students I found Nadia.

She had indeed been his wife, but much more important than that she had witnessed momentous events and great spiritual treasure—and it's this spiritual gold I want to share with you now. This is what makes Nadia's story such an important chapter. So don't tarry a moment longer, come and share an adventure through time.

***

(You can visit your other lives as often as you wish. They are quite solid. They do not melt away after you've had a look. They are like stations on a train line, linked by the rails (the rails being the journey of your soul), but they are all quite separate destinations you can choose to stop off at, at anytime. It would be third time lucky with this visit. I'd reviewed this life first with the student to look at the husband-and-children side of things—later with Ye in Whitley Bay to focus on Jesus's teachings for the Mind Body Spirit talk—and now I was about to revisit the memories with Veronica as part of the research for the book. Veronica's persistence would bring out the story of the miser—probably why the tapes had gone missing.)

***

The session began.

We lit a candle and drew the soft, translucent, white velvet curtains of my beautiful healing sanctuary.

Relaxed on my therapy couch, cozy with blankets and pillows, and with the hushed strains of soothing music whispering away in the background I shut my eyes. I focus on Veronica's voice as she detaches me from ordinary reality and takes me into the inner world.

I visualize descending a staircase and meet with my inner guides. As you'll remember Frances is my main guide and I've been aware of him ever since I learned about guides, but another guide, Hera is helping with the research for my writing, and on this occasion, Jesus is with them. He knows exactly what I need to remember, and so I enter the inner world's hallway of doors. I am drawn to a golden door set in a golden door frame, complete with lever handle and a golden key. It is a very heavenly looking door with white-gold light escaping around the edges, and I know passing through the light will cleanse me and that I need no other protection

I stand in front of the door.

I visualize turning the key.

I open the door and step through—into baking sunshine... It's very hot. It's very dusty. I'm in Damascus market, in the land of Syria, *but I've stepped back two thousand years.*

I'm now Nadia, daughter of nomad traders... and I'm nearly sixteen.

NADIA'S Story

As I look around me in the heat and dust there are people and camels everywhere. My tribe is here, and we've brought our spices, and seeds such as cumin, fine fabrics, and all manner of textiles to trade. It's very busy. It's very noisy. Voices rise and fall... haggling, bargaining.

I'm helping my parents sell their cloth.

I love the excitement of markets!

After the long boring silence of the empty days in the desert, it's fun to be in the midst of such noisy crowds. All around me bargain hunters are searching the goods strewn across blankets spread out on the dusty ground—and Damascus has to be my favorite market. It's where the trade roads cross. Not just one ancient trade road goes through here, camel train after camel train passes through, so you never know what you're going to see from what far-off places—or who you're going to meet—and you certainly don't know what you're going to hear. Just as much as the goods that we bring, the market is our place to exchange news and stories—and I can hear lots of laughter spicing the conversations around me. But today the market is buzzing with talk of a teacher, and I've never heard the like before.

A teacher?

Market gossip says this teacher is traveling around the area giving talks, and the next one will be at the end of the day's trading. It's going to take place in the outer courtyard of the main temple. People my family know, other traders we've bumped into at different markets over the years, keep saying the same thing to us, telling us, "He's good, you know, you ought to go along there tonight."

...And throughout the day a steady stream of people mention this talk, saying, "Don't just dash off after the market finishes. It won't be for long."

By the time the tenth trader whose opinion my father respected had said the same thing to him, and said how good the teacher was, we all become very curious. You just don't get people giving talks, as it's nothing to do with putting money in the purse or food in the stomach. Not *giving* them. And that's how my mother, father, his brothers and some of *their* families, and I all decide we will go along to see for ourselves what it is about.

It is our custom to eat after we finish trading for the day, so we plan to take our food with us and have it in the temple courtyard instead of by the market. Those of our tribe not interested in going to the talk agree to stay behind with our camels and goods and promise to wait for us under the palm trees.

***

As the day wore on a sense of anticipation grew inside me. I'd never had a teacher of any sort before, and I wondered what it would be like. My parents had taught me everything I knew, and that was mostly about cooking and helping with children. I was familiar with the history of our tribe (as it was talked about around the campfires at night), but I'd never been too interested in the spiritual code of beliefs of my people. Boys have more of an education in that, although I do understand we're all children of the great Creator and that there's a purpose to things. I'd traveled through many countries in my life, because we're always on the move, and I'd noticed that people called their gods by different names and that they gave water different names too. But it always seemed to me that it amounted to the same thing really—be it Jupiter, Baal, or Zeus—just like water is water, whatever name you choose to call it by.

...I was not normally one to get lost in my thoughts.

My day-to-day life was basic, and it had trained me to live in the moment through my senses. My days were all about camels and eating. I needed my camel to travel on, and what made the difference between life and death was having something to eat and water that was safe to drink. But that afternoon, as the shadows of the palm trees lengthened, I couldn't keep my mind from wandering.

The evening, when it came, was still hot.

***

The journey to Damascus had been tiring and the day's trading had been long and hard, and so it was with weary footsteps that we made our way toward the temple in the late afternoon. As we walked I looked behind me and saw other traders drifting out of the market and following on behind us. There were people from the city itself making their way to the temple too, and soon everyone was crowding into the outer courtyard. Temple guards indicated where we were to wait, waving us over to the left-hand side.

My family settled themselves down and got comfortable on the sun-warmed stones of the courtyard's floor, and then we got out our food. The market had been too busy for us to eat much during the day, and we were really hungry now. The food was quickly passed round and the bread, cold lamb, cheese, grapes, and dates shared out. There was water to drink, but some of the men had wine.

We were all glad of the rest and began to relax and unwind after the day. Finishing off the sweet and crunchy grapes we'd bought at the market I licked juice from my fingers, and feeling a bit bored, I idly stretched out my right foot, twisting my ankle from side to side to admire the ankle bracelet that now jingled and tinkled there. I'd longed for one like this for years.

My sandals and harem trousers were old and worn, the cuffs softly fraying, but this bracelet was brand new. Its bright silver lay against my nut-brown skin and as I watched the play of the fading sunlight on the shiny metal my face was one big smile. I loved dancing. And from now on whenever I stamped my feet, as I danced beneath the stars by the light of the campfires, all the little dangling bits that hung from it would make a pleasing sound. But I couldn't help the thought sneaking in that two would have looked so much better ... because they were usually worn as a pair.

I had often pestered my father for a set of these bracelets, but he would say, "Ooh... they're very expensive, and you're not very old yet, when you're older..." but today he had produced this as a surprise gift and I was thrilled. Unfortunately, and to my great dismay, he'd said I would have to wait a couple of years for the other one, but when he'd got the money we'd come back for it.

I'd done my best to hide my disappointment. I loved my father. I knew he worked very hard, and that whenever he made money he lavished it on our family and never kept much for himself. He'd bought gifts for my mother and for my younger brothers and sisters as well, and I sighed because I knew I was lucky to have even the one. I had to admit I'd had more than my fair share as it was...

A stir ran through the courtyard and I stopped admiring my bracelet for a minute to look around. People had arrived, a whole party of people. The teacher was there and his men were beginning to clear a pathway for him through the throng now packing our side of the courtyard. Everyone was in a relaxed and jolly mood and cheerfully shuffled aside to let the men pass. My sharp eyes took in their clothing. I had an eye for fabrics as they were the stuff my family's fortunes rested on. We made our living by traveling, buying them here and selling them there—wherever they fetched a better price—and all my life I'd been on the move and so I'd come to know the variations of weave, color, and cut in the different localities.

I could read their clothing as others would read a map.

Though the teacher was simply dressed I could tell that his helpers came from many different places. Yes, there were local people from Damascus with him, but others had traveled quite a distance—and by the looks of it they had joined his party as he passed through various villages and towns along the way. Some of the men were big and burly, considerably taller than he was, and they gave the impression of being body guards. There was something about their manner that made me wonder if they were expecting trouble. Most of them stayed at the back, near the guards, who were busily policing the main thoroughfare through the courtyard.

By contrast the teacher looked very peaceful. His hair was a considerably lighter brown than my thick dark tresses. It was straight with a parting and shorter than mine, and he had a small beard. He did not have a hawkish-looking "strong face," or simply a handsome face, but it was a lovely face, calm and very kind looking, with nice eyes, nose, and mouth. He was a young man of around thirty, it was hard to tell exactly how old he was, but he was old enough to know what he was doing and not old and wrinkly like the priests with the great big beards.

I saw some of the people with him giving little bags of money to the temple guards to allow this gathering to happen. Ragtag travelers like us and ragamuffins from the market were not usually welcome at the temple unless money changed hands, and the guards made it clear we would all have to go before the main business of the temple started later that evening. Those who brought offerings to the temple and the sort who paid money for the birds in cages for sacrifice would be arriving then.

As soon as the teacher began to talk, the people with him sat down on the floor in front of him, facing the crowd, and a few of the taller ones stood behind him, as though protecting him, possibly for the benefit of the guards, or for anybody who might try to break up the meeting. As he spoke a hush descended, and even the caged birds went quiet.

He greeted everyone. He had a pleasant voice, not loud and booming, but I could hear it clearly and it was gentle and loving. And it was love he talked about.

He said how important it is. He began:

> "Behold the beauty of the evening sky above us. God, our father, paints it crimson now in preparation for the twinkling of the stars of night to come. We live in a world of so much beauty, and He wants to share it with us.

> "There is beauty that the eye can behold but there is also beauty of the spirit within"—and here he touched his heart—"that spark inside us that is our link to God, our holy father, He who paints the heavens. He has touched my heart and charged me to share the beauty of the spirit within *you*, His children.

> "He causes the rains to fall and brings seed time and harvest, and so we have nourishment for our bodies. But He also wants us to have nourishment for our spirits. He has touched my heart and charged it with a message to share with you here tonight. And that message is about love. For love is the food of the spirit. With love it will prosper and thrive, and without it, it will shrivel and die. It is simple and it is simply said."

Love is the only thing that really matters, and though you've been busy doing trading, those of you from the market—the only thing that really matters is the love that you trade, with those who are with you, with people you come into contact with. It's not about gold or goods, although that's a part of life, it's the love that we all trade that's really important. That's what's important to my father in heaven, who is your father too, who is the great, kind, wise, and loving God who brought the world into existence and who gave us our lives, and who looks after us in our lives and welcomes us back into His heavenly home when we die, when we depart this life.

***

He said that some of this love from his father was inside each and every one of us, that it was in our hearts, and we needed to feel it and find that love and let that love *grow* and flow out through our words and deeds, through our hands, through our breath, through our feet, just *through* us as we expressed it into the world. "Can you feel this love inside you?" he asked, and as he spoke I could.

He told stories about families with love and families that lacked love, and what happened and how it affected the people. I could see from what he was saying that in the families where love flowed things were much better, happier, and things turned out better and were more prosperous as well. This was because although love is what counts, it is an energy. Gold is also an energy, and gold and love are the same but different. **Love is the gold of the spirit, and gold is the gold of the world**. When you have the riches of the spirit you can also attract the riches of the world, but if you only have the riches of the world they are dead, and you will be dead inside because you haven't got the love to give you life.

***

You may think you need a hundred camels or a hundred sacks of gold, but the only thing you really need is love. There is a love-shaped hole within our hearts and the only thing that can fill it is love. It can't be filled with camels and sacks of gold although they're valuable in their own way and they do other things. They will never, ever, fill the love-shaped hole in our hearts.

We have the love from the father in our hearts and we have a hole for more love, and this is the love we need to gather and we need to give. We can receive it from other people and they can receive it from us, so there should be a flow of love, we should all be helping each other to fill that hole, and that's what happiness is. It's nothing to do with camels and sacks of gold. But if you have that love in your heart then you're generous with your camels and sacks of gold, and your generosity spreads like a tide in the world, and it comes back to you as well, many times over.

***

I understood that he was saying everyone was better off when we are loving, and I enjoyed all the stories he told to illustrate this. I wondered if he'd made some of them up, but they were a good means to communicate the truth of it, and they made it easy to understand what he meant.

***

And the next day, when my younger sisters were pestering me to tell them one of the teacher's stories, I had rooted about in my few belongings to find one of my little treasures with which to illustrate his story for them.

I produced a fluffy iridescent feather I'd found on the floor of the market, and then went over to the remains of the campfire and fished out a small, blackened, bent stick. I did my best to remember how the teacher's story had started. I began by saying, "There once was a miser who hoarded his gold..."

The story had told how in his concern that no one stole it from him he had hidden it away, but so successfully that he could never find it again. He had spent all the rest of his life eaten up by the crossness and loss, it had soured all the years of his life in the world until he died. Then he went to meet the heavenly father, who said, "Welcome my son, what have you brought me from the gift of your life that I gave you?" and the miser said, "I worked really hard and got all this gold and put it somewhere safe, but then I couldn't find it." The heavenly father replied, "Well, the gold is of the world, so it's still in the world and it's not something you can ever bring to me, so what did you do with my gift of all those other years?" And the miser said, "I was trying to find the gold." He had not married or had children, he had not loved. What he'd done had twisted him up and there he was now, standing before God, a little, starved, blackened, twisted soul, charred by his crossness and anger, shriveled from lack of love. Here I waved my stick about before continuing, "And his heavenly father was thinking, 'Is that all?' 'So you went into life as a beautiful fluffy soul,'" I waved the pretty feather about, "'And you got your gold, but now you've come back as this little, thin, twisted, blackened soul. Is that really all you've done with my gift?'" I paused dramatically, playing for time as I tried to remember the ending.

"Ooh!" chimed my sisters. "What *does* God do with him now?"

I opened my mouth and was about to say there was no place in heaven for someone like him, such a miserable old stick, but I knew that wasn't quite right, tempting though it was. I thought hard and cast my mind back to the courtyard. I pictured it bathed in the fading evening sunlight, and I tried to remember the teacher's voice. And then I had it.

I knew God had to find him somewhere to go, and I continued the story. I said he didn't get thrown out of heaven, but he had had to go into a place with other twisted charred souls until he was ready to understand the need to change, because until this point he hadn't seen why it wasn't a good idea to do what he did.

I remembered the teacher had said that our heavenly father has infinite patience, and His home has many mansions. It is so big there are places for *everybody* at whatever level they are at, whatever state they are in.

"But if you go into a place you're not ready to go into, well, you won't find it comfortable," I told my sisters. "So if a twisted black stick soul went into a room with fluffy feathery souls it would feel very odd and lonely, and this would not help it to grow, so it has to go with its own kind and then they will all feel at ease and they can begin their journey onward when they're ready."

My sisters clamored to know what the souls did in the mansions.

I said I wasn't exactly sure, but it wasn't so much about doing things there, as just being. I closed my eyes for a moment and tried to recapture the feeling I'd had when the teacher was telling us about the mansions. I said, "You know before you sink into sleep, when you're full of peace and feeling still inside, when you've forgotten the world and you feel like you're sinking slowly into a golden pinkness—well, that's what it's like in the heavenly home. But just as you don't sleep forever, even in heaven there comes a time when you get restless." I suspected the "sticks" got restless rather quickly and didn't get to enjoy a long rest in the heavenly home, but I pressed on with the story, trying to keep to the spirit of the words as I'd heard them.

I explained God knew there would come a time when those "stick" souls would want to grow and change because they were discontented where they were. They would want another life, and then He would help them into the gift of a new life hoping that they'd learned something from their previous one. Then at the end of the new life they would come back to Him, and perhaps this next time they would be bringing a little bit more love and have done something else with the gift of the years that He had given them ... and over the following days, I really did my best to share what I'd heard with my sisters ...

***

But back in the temple courtyard the teacher still had my full attention.

He'd come to the part where he explained that you don't get punished, you punish yourself. That what you've selected and chosen has determined what you are, and he said that we are all responsible for ourselves and we make our own journey. We make it long and hard, or short and easy, depending on how much love we let ourselves enjoy. He said:

> My father's home has many mansions so everybody can find a place where they are suited, where they are comfortable with the level they have reached—and then they have a chance to ride on the river of love that is always flowing out from the heavenly father to all His children. It flows out from His heart and His mind, it flows out from the depths of His being and it carries us with it into the world of form with the gift of our new life in the world.

> And then you have all those years of that gift, to gather experiences and to weave your own pathway, and to dance, and to sing, and to love, and to do all those things that you choose. You can nurture your spirit and you can gather and give love, and you can ride that tide of love until on your last day you come back, the river of love brings you back into the depths of your father, into the mansions of the heavenly father, and He says, "Welcome my child, what have you brought Me from that gift I gave you of the years and the days of your life?"

> Then He listens, as a father listens to a son returning from a journey. And He is filled with joy for the successes and weeps about the bad

things, and puts His arms around you and welcomes you back. Then you move into one of the mansions, and then when you're ready, when you begin to feel like you want to experience more, you want to grow, you want to change, then you go back, sailing on that river and into the world to another life, another chance to gather love, to perfect love, to develop yourself as a loving being.

***

I realized that the teacher was saying we were not to be afraid of dying, **it's simply going home**, going to meet our heavenly father who loves us more than any earthly father can. He doesn't punish us. We may have punished ourselves, but He'll always help us. He doesn't judge us, but He really wants the best for us. So we get endless opportunities of bettering ourselves, of being more loving. The more love we have, the more comfortable we are when we're with Him. The less love we have, the less comfortable we are when we're living with Him, because He is pure love. So if we haven't got much love within us, then we're in the outer reaches of the mansions because we're just not comfortable nearer to Him.

And the trick to having love is giving it. If you give it you begin a flow, even if you just start by giving it to a plant or an animal. By admiring a sunset you are giving love to the world.

And here the teacher held his arms out wide to the darkening sky.

***

He had been a charismatic speaker talking with passion and conviction. He had made his words come alive. He spoke to the crowd as though he knew each and every one of them, as though he was looking into their hearts and could see their very souls as he was speaking. People had been quiet and still as they listened, and curiously at times it had seemed as though his words were meant for them alone, as if he was reading their mind and their heart and he knew what it was they needed to hear.

But when he had reached this point in his talk the last of the light was draining from the sky and the temple torches were being lit. He stopped to allow water to be passed out from big pots, and people were glad of it because of the heat. But then the guards signaled it was time to bring the talk to an end.

The teacher looked around at everybody and smiled.

He said: "Love your animals and your children, your crops and your camels. The whole world was brought into being from love from the heavenly father. It was given to you as your home and you should love it, respect it, nourish it, and care for it. You should love the world and treasure all the things in it because they're your gift from the heavenly father.

"He wants the best for you, and He has sent me to help you to understand Him. To help you to understand how much He loves you, and how important it is that you bless yourselves with love, that you fill your lives with love, that you express love and receive love, and that you are in your home, the one that He has given you, in a loving manner. And *that's* how you should conduct yourselves, *with love*. Be kind to strangers, kind to animals, kind to your nearest and dearest and to your family."

***

The teacher paused.

Looking at the upturned sea of faces in front of him, he said that though we had to go now, he wanted to give everyone a blessing for their journey out into the world. And stretching his hands out toward us he spoke:

May the light of my father go with you,

May His love ever shine in your heart,

May love guide your tongue and your footsteps in this world,

Until you rest in the peace of His heart.

***

As soon as he'd finished, those who had come with him, who were sitting on the floor in front of him, stood up, and he was swept out of the courtyard at the center of a phalanx of his followers. I saw some of the richer ones giving more coins to the guards on their way out, as a "thank you."

Then he was gone.

And it was time for the people to gather up their things.

They began to stream out of the courtyard, and my family walked back to our camels near the market.

My head was spinning with love as I walked. There was so much to think about and it had all made so much sense. All the things he'd said about love made me long to have children and a husband of my own to love and to practice loving with. I did love my camel, but when we got back to the camels I saw my mother's camel waiting there too. It was a sour old beast with a haughty air, and it still remembered my childhood tricks and teasing. It was a boss camel with a high standing among the others because it was the mother of so many of them, including my own, and it would sometimes nip me and spit. It was certainly not sour with everybody, but I laughed as I realized I was even going to have to try to love that one now.

My father was saying, "Well, what did you think? Did you enjoy that? Was it worth going?"

And I told him it was. I said, "It was very important and I'm glad I went."

But I grew impatient as my father seemed in no hurry to move off.

I said, "Shall we go now?"

He said we had to wait a minute, and he went round checking the camels and finished tying up things in the luggage before finally confessing he was waiting for somebody to come for one last trade. "Have a bit of patience, Nadia," he said to me. "Just wait a minute."

It wasn't long before we could see people hurrying toward us, a plump trader huffing and puffing behind a couple of his young apprentices. He panted up to my father and gasped, "I've got it here for you, if you've got the money," and he produced a small package. When this final trade was completed I discovered that the waiting had been for my benefit all along, and that the trade was for the other bracelet for my other foot!

The trader had had to go back to his workshops to collect it, he'd sent word earlier that his apprentices were to finish making it, and now he'd come back with it. So I had the matching pair I'd longed for and was ecstatic. It really was a wonderful day. I'd wanted these for ages and now at last they were mine, and I'd heard all that beautiful teaching. I knew I'd got a lot of treasure that day—I had treasure in my heart and treasure on my ankles!

I thanked my dad and gave him a big hug. I thought he really was a good dad and if my heavenly father loved me as much as my dad, well, it was just a wonderful thing.[31]

***

By this time it was dark, so with everything now complete we mounted our camels and began moving off into the night. It was cooler traveling under the stars, and we wanted to get out of the city to find somewhere to pitch tent and settle down for a few days.

The next day much was said about the talk. Those who had been to it were very impressed, and told everyone else in the tribe that if they got the chance again, if they came across the Nazareen a second time, they needed to go and hear him. And this was why my little sisters had pestered me to see what they'd missed out on and to discover what all the fuss was about.

When we mentioned his name to other people we met along our way, we found a surprising number had heard of him, and those who'd met him said, "Yes, he's very good, it's a good thing to listen to that Jesus, him from Nazareth."

I often thought about his words as my camel plodded away through the long days of the caravans. He'd said, "Life is beautiful but some men make it ugly," and as we traveled I saw people living this out, causing pain and suffering to others, all because they themselves suffered from lack of love. Had they just given a bit of love out, I thought, they'd have got twice as much back because that's the magic of love, it expands and expands.

---

31 Nadia's father had made a bargain with God. The night his wife's time came to be delivered of their first child he had promised to love and cherish it, boy or girl, if only God would spare her and not take her from him in childbirth. He had kept his side of the bargain, and repeated it each time they were blessed with children. Two daughters had followed Nadia before his sons were sent to him, but he did truly love them all, and they knew it.

(But I will point out that life is not a fairy tale, and though my father did love my mother there were plenty who thought that my mother was much like her camel, and not without reason. Walking back from the temple when I had been saying I wanted a husband of my own, my father cautioned me not to be in too much of a rush to find a husband … because it was a long time to rue a mistake …)

I thought about my tribe. I decided we were quite a loving people to start with, and perhaps that was one of the reasons we were always on the move. We saw bad things in the townships and bad things in the villages, bad things on the way even—people not being kind. Sometimes we rescued people and took them with us, like when we freed people's slaves who were being given a bad time, and then they weren't slaves anymore when they were with our tribe. Of course we were accused of stealing them...

It was true to say my people represented a threat to those who sought to control, which was why we were not always liked. The things we brought were liked, the salt, the silks, and all the other things, but our destabilizing influence was not. We were a completely free people. We were the Moving People and we lived on a tide, like a restless river, always moving. And this was the way I would meet my husband-to-be, when the tribe came across two runaways and took them with us.

Chapter 9
The Promise

NADIA'S Story Continued

Soon after Damascus I'd fallen in love and met the man I wanted to marry. Our union was blessed with two children in quick succession. They grew strong and healthy and I was happy, very happy. Unfortunately, my man's cousin was to cause us trouble, but at this time life was still good. The trouble came later, as you will hear.

But what is more important, we met Jesus again.

Time had passed.

***

(In this part of the regression I got the impression that Jesus's ministry was longer than the three years usually allotted to it; I know I'd had my children before we were to encounter Jesus the second time. At the time of his teaching on the mountain that you're about to hear about, they were too young to understand his teaching, but old enough to be left behind for a few days with the other children of our tribe.

As you know, the Bible tells us that Herod ordered babies two years and under killed in an attempt to kill the infant Jesus. Herod died in 4 BC, so it is thought that Jesus was likely born 6–4 BC, but it's not to say the baby-killing command came at the exact end of Herod's life. It could have happened earlier—meaning Jesus could easily have been born earlier. Conventionally, Jesus is regarded as having preached and gathered followers around AD 27–29, and then continued until being crucified some time between AD 30 and AD 38, certainly before AD 39.

This means Jesus could well have been over forty when he died.[32] I don't suppose we will ever know for sure because the surviving records from that time are patchy. So bear with me and understand that I'm talking very loosely when I say a few years passed, probably somewhere between three and seven, before we ran into Jesus again.)

***

On our endless journeying we passed through a village in Judea and went to the inn for food and water, and it was then we found that the Nazareen and his party were there. It was only because we had heard him teach at Damascus that we knew who he was, and we went up to him and said what a good teaching it had been.

I still had a lithe dancer's body, and I snaked my way through the crowd that was gathering around him. I wanted to get near him.

He was a gentle person with a peaceful, loving face, and I could not imagine him ever getting cross. He radiated a deep peace, and I found it a nice feeling to be standing so close to him. I noticed he made people peaceful even if they were as jangly as my bracelets when they came up to him. He had a very calming effect, and I could see that those with him were very protective and adored him.

Jesus said he wanted to give the tribe a blessing, and that we were to take what we'd heard at Damascus out into the world and share it with others, because that really was what was important—**what we do with the years of our life, and what we take back to our heavenly father**.

Then he went outside to where our camels were waiting, and he blessed the camels and even the trading goods on them. He said that the goods were important, although they were not as important as love, but it was important to have sustenance in the world, like love is sustenance for the spirit. Then he blessed our tribe, saying:

> *May you be strong and thrive, and may you take my words out into the world. May you be protected by the heavenly father as you go about your lives, and may you never forget the message about love. May you share it with many people along the way, and while you do that you will always be protected, you will be safe, and misfortune will not come to you.*

---

32   St. John (8:57): *"The Jews therefore said unto him,* **Thou art not yet fifty years old,** *and hast thou seen Abraham?"* This could indicate Jesus was nearer fifty than we might think—in his forties, say—rather than a youthful thirty.

After that the whole tribe did feel truly blessed, and very fortunate that he had made time for us. We knew he was a busy man, always on the move, taking his message out to people, traveling round his country— although he didn't travel afar like we did, on the long journeys to Egypt and beyond.

He told us he was planning to do some big teachings in deserted places so that he wouldn't be moved on, as he had been at the temple. We could be there for days, a week or more, perhaps even ten days, he said, and we would be most welcome if we wanted to join in.

We were given the location, a mountain plateau, so if it was anywhere near our trading routes we could come along, and no matter how many of us wanted to come we would all be very welcome. He said,

> *You will need to bring food and water because it is going to be for a long time and there is not much up on the mountain, but everybody will be sharing and it is going to be like a festivity, a celebration. I will be leaving for a while shortly afterwards, and so this will be a sort of "goodbye" party, and I will be giving you more words to take out into the world and more food for your souls and spirits, more spiritual sustenance. It will be very beautiful and you will be most welcome. I am just doing what I have to do, and if you enjoyed hearing me before I think you will enjoy hearing me this time. The invitation is there should you wish to come, and you can give it to other people you meet, anybody who loves me, anybody who loves my teachings and my words is very welcome to come to the celebration before I go.*

***

Something about his words made me wonder. Was he saying he might be going back to his heavenly father and that his time of teaching was coming to an end? It was a bit mysterious, and there was an urgency about him that conveyed it really would be worth the effort to go.

The teaching on the plateau was planned for some months ahead, so there was time to fit it into the pattern of our customary journeys. And after some discussion we decided to go.

This time a lot more of the tribe elected to hear Jesus's words, but not everyone was interested, and it was no problem finding people to stay behind to look after the camels when the time came.

It was quite a climb up the mountain to the plateau, even for my strong young legs, but once I was there I had a really wonderful time. We were given simple white garments to wear, just tied at the waist with a cord, so that whatever our wealth or social standing we all looked the same—because we were all equal in the eyes of the heavenly father, Jesus had said. Those who had come shared what they'd brought. My people shared their spices, and that made the food tastier, and everyone was jolly and kind. The rich were giving away blankets, and they'd brought extra food too. Because they had money they were using it as love and they were helping others.

"There are some really lovely people here," I thought, and I felt touched deep inside. This was a way of looking at the world that was so different to what I normally encountered… a completely different way of being *in* the world. It was like the whole world was your family, and a really loving family at that.

Jesus did a lot of talking over the days, but he also had us moving about and doing things. As well as meal breaks, the days were broken up with dancing to get us moving and the joy flowing.

Beautiful music was provided by the musicians who'd come, and with all the words that had been said and all the things that we'd been told, I really wanted to meet my heavenly father so much that as I danced I lifted out of my body and found angels welcoming me, pulling me up and dancing with me. I'd always loved dancing, which was why I'd wanted the ankle bracelets, but now I was dancing on two different levels at the same time. As my body danced on the Earth below, my soul and spirit[33] were dancing with the angels above. It was just so joyful, they were laughing.

I soared above the plateau, and I could see that there were throngs of angels all around the mountain, all around the land, all in the sky—there were thousands upon thousands of them, tiers and tiers of circles of angels stretching up into the heavens. I was absolutely stunned. I hadn't seen them while I was watching Jesus and listening to him, but now I was out of my body I was in their world, and I realized there were a lot more angels there than people. They were singing, not like people sing, but they emitted a beautiful harmonious sound. They were singing the glory of the heavenly father, they were singing the glory of His son, they were singing the glory of all the children of the heavenly father. They were celebrating and so happy. Earlier, Jesus had been

33 Perhaps I should say "astral body," but "soul and spirit" was what was on the session tape.

telling us about angels, and all the children of the heavenly father that we couldn't see, and here they were.

Then I came back into my body, but I didn't forget what I'd seen. After the joyous dancing we lay down to rest, and it was after this that Jesus gave a short talk. He broke the news that this was going to be the last night on the mountain, and he said he'd like to have a little private farewell with everybody before he left, so if we'd like to do that, then this evening we could come up to him one by one and have some private words. He thanked everyone very much for coming and sharing the days with him, these days of the gift of the heavenly father, of our life.

We set up the fires and cooked the last meal, and it was quite a feast as now there was no need to hold food back. After we'd eaten, the farewells began.

Near the edge of the plateau there was a suitable area that offered a little privacy, where some rocks formed a jagged screen. Behind the screen a natural rock formation provided a seat with a back for Jesus, and in front of it a stool for the other person.

The queue started to form near the screen and nobody was in a hurry, and nobody was pushing to be at the front. Everybody was very gracious and everybody knew they would get their turn.

By the time my family took their place in the queue it was night and the delicate crescent of the old moon was set among the stars. The stars looked so beautiful in the vast darkness of the sky that I couldn't help but admire their twinkling brilliance and the mystery of the heavens, and then I thought of the heavenly father. I looked around me at the sky and the landscape and marveled. It was indeed a very beautiful home that he had prepared for His children.

And when it came time for my turn I sat down on the rock before Jesus. He took my hands in his and looked deep into my eyes. He said,

> *Take my words out into the world. You've listened, and you've shared, and you've been a part of things, and you've opened your heart. Take my words out into the world. Will you promise me to do that?*

***

And I replied with all my heart, "Yes, I will," for I was most certainly willing to do that for him. But at the same time another message had been given to me, transmitted through his gaze and laid down at a deeper level of my being, on the level of soul. The hidden message ran:

> *I know that you will have many tribulations, as the pathways through the world are not easy for the children who try to follow the message, but know that you will always have help, you will not be alone even though you may think it. And there may be many travails before the time comes when you take my words out to a bigger audience, but the time will come, and you will know when it comes, and you will have all the help that you need. You need to open your heart and share the truth, the truth about love, and that is what will set mankind free and break the bonds which tie you all to the bad things from the past,[34] it will free your spirits so that you may live in a golden future, one that makes our heavenly father smile, one that brings love to flow freely into the world as His children live in the manner to which they were destined when they were created. Open your heart and share the words that will help the plan of Creation unfold within those who listen and heed the message; share the words that can be a compass and a map to a golden future.*

***

And when I say "yes" to the message I hear, I am also saying "yes" to the one that is hidden within me, one that would be carried by my soul through many lifetimes before the time spoken of came to pass. This was part of a spiritual contract arranged before my birth, and it was the very reason for my incarnation. My consent freely given grounded the soul's intention on Earth.

Under the light of the stars in the heavens I kissed Jesus's hands and went to rejoin my family. I settled down with my bedroll and prepared for sleep, and as I began to drift off I became aware I was floating out of my body again, and I could see the angels. They were still there and they were all still singing, and the two with big white wings, the very same two I had danced with before, were there again, pulling me up to dance in the stars. As I laughed in the ecstatic dance they communicated silently with my soul.[35]

---

34 And by this he meant what we now understand as "karma."

35 Laughter is music to God, and angels do find it hard to understand why we are so gloomy so much of the time. They just dance and sing and celebrate Creation. While we have to deal with earning a living and finding food! But when we dance our joy and love flows, and then it is much

They introduced themselves as the archangels Uriel and Raphael, and they undertook to help my soul with its deeper promise when the time came—and by that they meant helping this book come into the world. They promised to help with its purpose of spreading the truth for healing people. Uriel is ever the revealer of truth, and Raphael, the healer, would work through the words of the book that they might bring healing to people's minds and emotions. That is where, so often, the damage in the body first starts.

In their joy they took me to meet Gabriel. He undertook to help reinforce the strength of the message of **love**, because that is the most important thing. Its lack is the biggest poverty there is and its presence is the biggest treasure, and the only thing that is really real is love. And that is why they had come to me, because my soul would need to draw on their qualities to actually fulfill the future mission, the one that had been promised to Jesus.

With my head full of happy thoughts of angels and dancing I drifted off to sleep, and in the morning when I woke with the light, Jesus had already gone. He left after he had finished the farewells, and all his people were gone with him.

I looked down from the mountaintop and saw dust in the distance marking his progress.

Then there was nothing to do but to pack up, and perhaps people were a little bit subdued as they collected their things together. But it had been so wonderful everyone felt a deep joy inside and felt very, very lucky and very privileged to have been there. Then it was back on with ordinary life, but with that different viewpoint, a different way of looking at the transactions undertaken in the world, when we were talking to people and doing things.

***

It was as though Jesus lit a golden flame within the hearts and minds of people. Souls were touched and set on fire by his teachings. He made an all-out effort to reach as many people as possible in the short time that he had, and the profound effect of his incarnation is still with us as an echo in the words of the Bible, but many have been lost. Although they may be lost they are not necessarily forgotten, and many people have hidden treasure relating to Jesus and are still carrying his living

---

easier for higher frequency beings to reach down to us.

words in their soul memories.

But he had been right to call it a farewell party. All too soon came the traumatic end. The sky grew dark and the light went out of the world as Jesus was crucified, just like it says in the Bible. I and many of our tribe watched from afar, numb with horror and despair. We would have willingly traded our lives in his place, and the depth of our grief showed us what we had lost and just how much treasure Jesus had brought us.

I kept the promise I had made him and shared his words with others. When things had been bad or situations difficult, I'd always asked myself, "Where is the love in this? What does love tell me to do here?" And I'd done my best to use my heart as my compass to steer me through.

But I owe it to you to explain a little more of the difficulties I've hinted at in that life.

You know that my tribe had taken two runaways with them, and that one became my husband, but the other, to whom he'd been chained when we found them, was his cousin. The cousin was the cause of mischief. He had a possessing spirit inside him, which could make him angry and unpredictable. We bore with him on the road, but in towns he would often shout at the Roman soldiers and insult them, causing trouble. He couldn't seem to help himself. (This is why the pair of them had been briefly imprisoned, because although my husband had tried to prevent him causing harm he'd been locked up with him, deemed guilty by association.)

Eventually we could protect the poor man no longer when he enraged a soldier who ran him through with his sword. You could be excused for thinking that this might have been a blessing, an end to the trouble, but as my husband cradled his dying cousin in his arms he cursed him. "May you be at the Banquet of Life and be unable to eat," he spat, and with those words he died, and although we didn't know it, the possessing spirit migrated into my lovely man.

The cousin died before we met Jesus again, and Jesus's blessing on our tribe helped ameliorate the curse. But I can see now that we should have actually asked Jesus for healing over this. We'd been in denial, hoped it would go away, and tried to forget the hate-filled words of the angry man. But over the years the curse slowly sapped my husband's health.

It wasn't that he became angry and unpredictable, it hadn't changed him in that way, but it got harder for him to nourish his body and keep food down. This came to a head when our daughter was betrothed to be married in a peace-broking arrangement with another tribe. She was fifteen years old and happy with the match, excited to start her new life. Diplomatically it was a very auspicious and important union for our tribe. We were honored by this marriage, which is why we couldn't get out of it. My husband had to be at the feast and he had to be seen to take part, or it would have been a great dishonor for our tribe. But as the time approached, my son and I knew the rich food at the banquet would kill him.

He was very weak. We were desperate.

We carried him against his protestations into the desert, to a hermit healer—a wild-haired, wild-looking man who lived in a cave. We had been given his whereabouts by followers of Jesus we'd met along the way. And despite his wild appearance he helped us.

He drew the possessing spirit from my lovely man and trapped it in a stone bottle. He pushed in a stone stopper to seal it. "Leave it with me," he said—and gratefully we did. From that moment on my husband's strength and appetite returned. He grew strong enough for the wedding feast…

And all was well.

Life continued, and when the river of love finally brought Nadia to her last day and carried her back to the arms of the heavenly father, it was a mountain of love that she brought with her.

It is so important Jesus didn't die in vain.

What we do with his gift from now on is what counts.

**

The difficult person who had caused Ye to look at his past life felt like this cousin, and that explained a lot! He was still an angry, jealous man, whom Ye yearned to heal. Our getting married had raked up the old conflict, because we were together again. The session showed the size of the problem and how long it had been going on. Sometimes, for your own protection, you just have to back off and let people be. And although talk of possessing spirits may sound peculiar today, removing them was a big part of Jesus's healing ministry according to the Bible. Even today the Church has specialists who still do this work.

***

Recovering the memories of being Nadia has helped me tremendously in my life today, and I find the teachings a great comfort. I still love jewelry and dancing, but Nadia would have laughed in bemusement at the way I overthink things. She lived in a refreshingly simple and direct way that is good for me to remember.

But whatever life I've looked at in a regression I always have a profound sense of wonder as I get up off the therapy couch because:

- You never fail to learn something that is important for you.

- It explains so much about why you feel the way you do about things (and you find you're not as irrational as you may have thought, you've simply forgotten why!)

- It is so amazingly easy to remember, once you know how.

Chapter 10
People of the Message

MARY'S Story

What would follow a life like Nadia's?

Well, I'd been so affected by Jesus that my soul craved to know more of him. I took the shortest of breaks in the mansions of the heavenly father and was drawn swiftly into a life in the very early Christian Church. In this next life I lived at a time when people still remembered people who had actually witnessed Jesus's miracles firsthand and who still had all of Jesus's words to cherish. And for a while after he left us, as it says in the Bible, Jesus manifested physically to his followers. Yes, he did. I witnessed it. It ensured that the wicked winds of the world did not extinguish the flame he had brought to light our way to the heavenly father. It was a wonderful time to be in the Church.[36]

The parents I came to for this next life lived at the north end of the Sea of Galilee, and by now it was the second half of the first century AD. My parents were **People of the Message**, people who cherished the

36 Ten different appearances of the risen Jesus are recorded in the New Testament, but it is implied in the words of Luke (Acts 1:3) that there may have been other appearances of which we have no record. After forty days Jesus was seen to ascend into heaven. But it was years later that he appeared to Saint Paul on the road to Damascus and spoke to him as the risen Saviour; Jesus appeared in a great light and Paul was struck blind for three days in order to stop him from persecuting the Christians in Damascus. Through this divine intervention Saul of Tarsus became Saint Paul (Acts 9:3–9; Cor. 15:8; 9:1).

In my recollection Jesus's appearances did go on for a considerable period of time, years after the Ascension, but curiously he never looked any older. That Jesus rose from the dead is fundamental to the Christian faith, and it is spoken of as the act of (1) **God the Father** (Ps. 16:10; Acts 2:24; 3:15; Rom. 8:11; Eph. 1:20; Col. 2:12; Heb. 13:20); (2) **of Christ himself** (John 2:19; 10:18); and (3) **of the Holy Spirit** (1 Peter 3:18).

Good News that Jesus, whom they called **the Savior**, had brought to humankind. The house my parents lived in was a house where Jesus had sometimes been a guest while on his travels—at which time it had belonged to my grandparents. The house had been a safe haven for Jesus then, and as such was well known throughout the community of believers; the house had a fame of sorts. It was called *Bethesda*—meaning *house of mercy*, because it was a place of healing. My family were doctors, physicians, and on his visits Jesus had sometimes healed those who had come knocking on our door in need of help. My mother grew medicinal herbs in our garden and made remedies from them, sometimes steeping them in olive oil. Those who could pay were charged, but the remedies were freely dispensed to the poorest of people. It really was a *house of mercy*.

Bethesda, our house, was to be found in Bethsaida, a city at the north end of the Sea of Galilee. Bethsaida was built where the River Jordan flows down into the sea. This area really was the epicenter of what you might call "Jesus country." Remember, it was on the banks of the Jordan that John the Baptist had baptized Jesus when his ministry first began, and Capernaum—a town at the north end of the Sea of Galilee—was where Jesus based himself after he left Nazareth.[37]

Jesus performed many miracles in this area during his ministry. It was near Bethsaida that the feeding of the five thousand took place, and soon after that he walked on the stormy waters of the Sea of Galilee. The disciples Peter, Andrew, and Philip came from Bethsaida.[38]

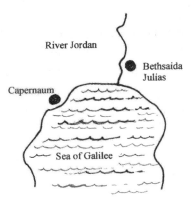

37 Matt. 4:13: "And leaving Nazareth, he came and dwelt in Capernaum, which is by the sea."
38 Luke 9:10; Mark 8:22, 6:45, Matt. 1:15–21, John 1:44, 6:17, 12:21. The Romans called the Sea of Galilee the Sea of Tiberius, and it is also referred to in the Bible as the Lake of Gennesaret, and in the Old Testament as the Sea of Chinnereth.

It's the memories of this life that I will share with you now.

But first a quick word about how this relates to my present life.

For a long time, I, Paulinne, had known I'd lived a life in the very early Christian Church. In fact, I had known about it ever since I'd met an acquaintance of Naomi's in 1984. The man had felt very familiar. It wasn't an attraction that I felt, but I knew I had known him before in another life. When I meditated on this I saw pictures of myself in a dark room with a square table, and I was opening my door to receive him as a visitor. In the old life he'd come burdened with questions for me to answer—questions about spiritual matters and about Jesus. Strangely enough he'd done the very same thing when I met him again two thousand years later. He'd questioned me closely on spiritual matters again, and once more he was Jewish while I was a Christian. Naomi, bless her heart, belonged to the Baha'i faith.[39] She had invited us both to the Baha'i Centre in Manchester to share in one of their celebration feasts. (Meeting him and answering his questions precipitated something important being restored to me, *the visual keys to contact God*, ancient training which I will be sharing with you, should you wish to try it. I find it excellent to decode dreams.)

But I was haunted by this picture in my mind's eye for years: the dark room with the square table. There were always flowers on the table and steps up to the door … in the picture he stood there in a long, coarsely woven, striped robe, like men wore in the East in those days. When I first wondered about my name, the name that came was "Mary of Bethesda," but also tantalizingly, "Mary of Bethsaida"—and at this stage I had no idea of the meaning or significance of the names. In fact, I was annoyed there were two! I thought it was some lack on my

39   The Baha'i faith is one of the youngest of the world's major religions. It was founded by Baha'u'llah in the nineteenth century. Baha'is believe that throughout history, God has sent to humanity a series of divine Educators—Manifestations of God—whose teachings have provided the basis for the advancement of civilization. These manifestations have included Abraham, Krishna, Zoroaster, Moses, Buddha, Jesus, and Muhammad. Baha'u'llah, the latest of these Messengers, explained that the religions of the world come from the same Source and are in essence successive chapters of one religion from God. Baha'is believe in the equality of the sexes, and that we are all eternal spirit. It is a monotheistic religion, and if you would like to know more check out their website: www.bahai.org.uk.

Baha'u'llah was born in Persia, which is now the Islamic country called Iran. In Iran Baha'is suffer severe persecution today, as Christians once did when they were perceived as a threat by Rome.

part that I couldn't pick the "right" one. But it was this mystery over the names that showed me there was more to find out if I got a chance to research it. ... But it never quite made it to the top of my list of things to check out—well, not until thirty-two years later—when I was readying *Spiritual Gold* to be a stand-alone book. You already know the reason for the names, but that was the trigger to research that life in the Holy Land to find its treasure. I hoped there was treasure.

I got more than I bargained for.

Because treasure there certainly was!

So that's why, on a blustery April day in AD 2016, Veronica, my hypnotherapist friend, was preparing me to enter the inner world once more. In the soft light of my healing sanctuary Veronica took me on the inner journey that was going to lead into my far memory.

***

The regression session began.

I relaxed on the therapy couch, comfy and cosy with blankets and pillows. I follow her instructions, which result in my detaching my awareness from the outer world and refocusing my awareness within. Veronica tells me to go to a special place in my inner world, a place where I can meet with my guides.

So I do.

I find myself in an ancient stone circle, like a small Stonehenge. My guides are already there: Frances is accompanied by Hera, and again I am aware of Jesus's gentle presence. Incongruously there's a strong, old, wooden door set in the largest of the stone circle's central post-and-lintel structures. The huge ancient stones form the door frame.

I know this is a portal.

I consider the door. It has panels and a white ceramic knob—there is no protective clothing to wear, but from the knob hangs a note that says,

Open me and be ready to receive the treasures within.

I know I have nothing to fear. I open the door and step through.

But I am no longer Paulinne.

Now I'm Mary—and I hear myself saying I'm Mary of Bethesda.

I look around…I'm standing on a dusty road. There is a donkey with me. I have a staff.

Overhead the midday sun is beating down from out of a cloudless sky. It's very hot, and my long black garments are streaked with the pale dust kicked up from parched stones that lie scattered on the surface of the road.

I've stopped to look at a town.

I'm outside this town now, leaning on my staff, just taking stock.

Looking.

I know this is Capernaum, this is my journey's end—and I can see buildings huddling and clustering together, all piled on top of each other, all leaning higgledy-piggledy against each other… and there are lots and lots of buildings… a souk… and a white dome. I've come here to start a new life in this place.

Veronica asks me how old I am.

Oh, I must be seventy-six, but it's hard to remember exactly how old you are when you're as old as I am! … I've been old for a very long time now… but I was young once!

Veronica asks if it's safe for me to be traveling on my own.

It's only a few miles and no one would bother an old woman like me on the road. That's why the donkey and I have walked here, and we've got here safe enough… My donkey is laden with two baskets, carrying all my worldly goods. What little I have is in them. At my age I don't need much, just a few clothes, a little water, some food and a cooking pot or two, and there's some money I've tucked away, concealed among my spices.

Veronica asks why I made the journey.

There's been trouble where I was living, so I've had to move on.

Bethsaida has been my home all my life, one way and another, but it's not safe for me now.[40] People I know have had their houses burned,

40 The old city of Bethsaida had been rebuilt and fortified around AD 30 by Philip the tetrarch, who called it "Julias," after the Roman emperor Augustus's daughter. (In Iron Age times

because of the trouble, and it was caused by jealous people gossiping. When I wrote to my friends at Capernaum to tell them what was going on they invited me to live in their community. So I sold up my house, Bethesda, bought the donkey, packed what little I needed, and walked here.

I've got strong bones and although I'm old, I feel young and happy inside. I've got plenty of spirit and it gives me joy. There's something very important that we share, these friends and I, we all share it, and it is *beautiful news*, that's what gives us the spirit and the joy inside. Someone very special gave it to us—the Savior. Officially he's been dead a long time now, but we treasure the Savior's Message of the beautiful news and keep it safe, beautiful news of the great, kind, and loving God whose children we are.

I wasn't here when he came; my grandparents were, and my parents were young back then. My family knew, my uncles and aunts too, so I was brought up with it. That's how I come to know about the Message. It makes you very joyful, but it doesn't always please people, especially not the people in power. They see us as a threat. So we have to be a bit secret. We laugh a lot and we're just so joyful sometimes that it gives the game away! And we don't do the things they expect us to do. We have another way of looking at things, and looking at money. We can't be bribed or cajoled and we don't take being threatened well. We have a knack of annoying people. We shine too bright. Although we put a cover over ourselves, they see the light through the chinks, and it makes them uncomfortable, and so we have to move on. We go, because we are free. There's no point staying and having a fight, it wouldn't serve any purpose. Because of what we believe we're not easy to control, and this is why there's trouble.

I've come to Capernaum because I've got family here, family in the Good News and actual blood family too. I'm bringing a bundle of letters with me—special letters written by the people left behind when the Savior went. They're for sharing with the community here, and I'm looking forward to hearing the letters they hold, when they're read out at our gatherings. Letters are very important to us, the special letters are cherished—they're not like the ones I write, that are just about

Bethsaida had spread out over twenty acres and had been a very important city. It was the capital of a kingdom back then, and on a trade route, but it had fallen into disrepair.) The land around the Jordan delta is very fertile, and Bethsaida's position made it important because of being on the trade route.

coming to stay.

I'm tired and it's hot.

So I sit down by the roadside beneath some shady trees.

I give the donkey food, and I eat a little bread and cheese myself, and some grapes. It's a very willing donkey, a good donkey. As we've walked the miles together, the donkey and I, I've talked to it, because I like it, and it understands the joy in my voice when I'm telling it about the Message. It might seem foolish but it makes me happy, and it makes the donkey happy too! So where's the harm in that? Eh, where's the harm in that?

***

When I arrive my friends meet me. I'm taken to one of the little higgledy-piggledy houses where I can leave my baskets and belongings. This is where I'll live from now on, this is a house for me now. The donkey is taken care of in a friend's stable. And then I'm taken on to a party—it's a feast of welcome! For me! And there's wine. Lots of lovely people have come and they tell me I'll be safe here, and that it's a good place to live, and they say they'll look after me, and that they are very pleased I've come to them.

It is so good to be among friends. And there is so much love in these people.

When I've met everyone they take me back to the little house that's now my home.

The house is below street level, in a very old part of town. The level of the road outside has risen higher over the years. Over the centuries, every time the road has been resurfaced it has risen, and because the house was built down a slope to begin with, it was always lower than the road. There's another dwelling built on top of mine.

I get into my house from the street by going down steps. I open the door and step down into my room. My room is quite dark because although it has a window, the window is greatly obscured by the shadow of the road outside. I can see the wheels of the carts as they rumble past, and people's feet. But there is a bit of light, and there is a big fireplace to my right. It's a square room and in the center is a big square table, solid and strong, and upon the table someone has put a clay jug filled with flowers—just wildflowers, flowers of the field. They never last long but it is such a kind thought. They look lovely, and seeing them brings me joy.

When I cross the room from the door, there's another door that goes into a simple little kitchen area where I can prepare food, and steps go up from this second door to my bedchamber above. So I have three rooms, plenty for my purpose—because I'm old, and I haven't got long, and it's just somewhere I can be at home, be at peace, and think about the Message. It will do me well. It's all I need now.

That night I'm tired, and there's no need to cook because of the feast, so I go to bed early.

I drift off to sleep easily because I always do, but I have an important dream.

In the dream the Savior comes, and he welcomes me and tells me I've been a good daughter of his Church, that's what he calls the People of the Message, his "Church."[41] It's just a very blissful experience in the dream, seeing him, being with him… and he holds my hand and says it's not long now and that I'll be with him soon. I'm so happy in the dream. He has my children with him and they're with me, in the dream… they're waiting for me. They died when they were young. It's hard to be children sometimes, a lot of them die… and my husband is there too. My husband, Ben, was a kind man, a man of the Message… So I've that to look forward to—and it won't be long, and then I'll be with them, and I'll be in the mansions of the heavenly father and the Savior will welcome me—well, that's what he's saying in the dream. It's a really beautiful dream. I wake up and I feel very happy.

Then it's the first day of my new life here in Capernaum.

People come knocking on my door, bringing me food—bread and other things—they're singing and so happy!

I think I'm going to be really happy here.

---

41   In the early Church the word did not mean the building in which they worshipped, because they had no churches. They just met in each other's homes. "Church" meant *the group of believers*— it was the people not the building. The word comes from the Greek "ecclesia," which means a called-out company, an assembly, a gathering, a body or organization. So "the Church" means the whole body of Christians, all the Christians in the world, even all the Christians who have ever been.

They want to take me around the town and show me places—like nice places to sit under the trees in the shade, where you can watch the world go by—and the market—and where to get food. Throughout the day the person with me changes, as people give up an hour of their day to help me get my bearings. It's very well organized, and the last one brings me back in time to make my evening meal, and they've made sure I have what I need for my cooking.

I make a chunky lamb broth with vegetables and herbs. I boil up lamb bones, the meat is finely chopped, and it all goes into one pot and cooks until the vegetables are meltingly soft. I haven't got many teeth left so it will be easy to eat and digest this. I don't need fancy stuff at my age! I rip up fresh bread and dip it in and suck the broth from it. I often cook this. It keeps my bones good and strong. I'm fit and sprightly. I don't ail like some people do.

And after the first dream I have many more good dreams that make me look forward to going to sleep each night. They are always a comfort to me, my dreams.

Over the months at Capernaum I often sit under the trees, the ones I was shown on the first day, and as I watch the world go by, I think about my life. I am happy here; I feel like everybody's grandma, like I've got lots and lots of children that like me and wish me well—and there's always someone dropping by with a little gift of food or to see how I am.

But we do this for everybody. It's just the way it is, because that is what we were told to do. Everybody is precious and valuable and equal, and we're all the children of God. So the biggest service we can do for God is to render a service to another of the children of God, and to do what we can to make them happy and well. It's very, very simple. And of course when you do that, you get the joy inside, so you're rewarded by that, and the person who's receiving is rewarded by the gift of the service, by the love and care that has been given. So the circle of joy always gets bigger!

And of course I help them too—I've done a bit of babysitting and that sort of thing. I know about healing herbs, so I help when children get sick. I had to learn quite a bit when my own children were young because they did struggle. I had a lot of children. Some died very young, others before they were ten years old—there are lots of dangers in life—bad water, spoiled food, diseases, accidents. But they didn't all die, my children; I had two sons who made a life for themselves in the world.

It's nice to be quiet now and then, and I only have to say if I want a bit of time on my own to think about my family. I miss them all, and I often think about them, but I'm never lonely here. And it won't be long...

I can still remember my parents.

They lived in Bethesda too; it was a good house with a courtyard garden, and it was there, in the garden, one evening that it all began. A late hen was wandering about scratching (I remember, because I love animals), but it was in the garden, under the stars, that Mum and Dad began reading to me and began sharing the Message.

I was twelve years old, so they knew I was old enough to understand the Message, and I found it beautiful—and they said that every night they'd tell me a bit more, and that they'd teach me to read and write for myself, so by the time I was grown, by the time I was ready to get married, I'd know all that I needed to know.

I gave them a big hug and a kiss and went to bed very happy that night.

As my father said, the day is for toil. But then we'd have our evening meal, and when the world was resting, when it was peaceful and quiet we'd sit in our garden. It was such a lovely place to sit. There was a little fountain, herbs, and a grapevine... and our rooms were arranged around the courtyard, all set out on a square.

When I was sixteen my parents found me a husband.

Ben was a friend of theirs. He was a farmer, and his family had provisioned my family with medicinal herbs for a long time. Although I was trained in basic wound lore and remedy preparation, my brother Reuben was apprenticed to my father and set to learn all his skills. Reuben worked with him, and was to take his place when Father died.

I had an uncle and aunt living on the outskirts of Bethsaida, much nearer to the River Jordan, and that's where Ben came from. I would stay with my uncle and aunt while we were courting, because it was hard for him to leave his animals and his farm. Ben was thirty-six. He was older than I was, so, as my parents said, he could provide for me. He was a good man who knew about the Message. Both of us knew, and so there was no conflict between us.

I lived on the farm with him when I was married, and then I was just plain Mary of Bethsaida, not Mary of Bethesda. But we were happy, and we made each other happy because we were doing what the Message said—making ever more love in our hearts, sharing it, and being kind—and when you do this love grows, and over the years it grows stronger. We had children, quite a lot of children, but most didn't live to grow up, only our two sons did, Peter and Paul. When my parents died our sons had our farm; they were young and strong, and we came back to live in Bethesda, my parents' old house. My brother Reuben had died untimely early, but I knew enough to offer a basic service and dispense the remedies myself. My husband grew old there and died.

I was a widow and I grew old myself, and everything was fine—until things got difficult when the trouble came.

Our sons had not been interested in the Message, not that they actually turned their back on it, but they didn't shine a very bright light, as you might say, so they were safe enough when the trouble started.

Nobody had pointed the finger at me, but I didn't feel safe because I knew it was just a matter of time. So I decided to go, and I sent a letter to Capernaum. When I got one back saying I'd be very welcome and that if I wasn't feeling safe I must come, I sold my parents' house. I sold it for a cheap price to a relative, another doctor in the family, to do him and his wife a good turn—it's a nice place to live, Bethesda—but I made them promise to continue dispensing the remedies freely to those too poor to pay. I even made them promise to only sell the house to people of the Message who would do the same when the time came for them to pass Bethesda on—so I did what I could to ensure that it continued to be a house of mercy.

***

One day I was in the back of my little house in Capernaum, cooking, when there was a fearsome knocking at my front door. I left the kitchen, and wiping my hands nervously I stood in my dark room and I looked at the door... There was nothing to be seen through the window—no Roman soldiers, or carts there—but I stood still and silent and frightened, my heart pounding, until a voice called out, "It's Mary I'm seeking, Mary of Bethesda. Mother, are you there?"

I gasped. It was Paul. I knew that voice.

I unbarred the door and there he was, I could see his feet and his long striped robe, and as I craned my neck and squinted against the light I could see his face.

I received my son in my arms. He was distraught. His brother Peter had died.

"We were very close in life, Peter and I, and I miss him—and I miss you—and I have no comfort. Is he safe with the Savior?" Paul asked, near to tears, in a voice cracking with emotion.

"I dreamed so," I replied.

"Tell me more about the Savior. I've turned my back on these things, and now I must know what it is I've scorned through fear. Tell me, Mother. Tell me now."

And so I did.

He cried and held me.

He confessed his new wife had died in childbirth, taking the baby with her. She had suffered the same fate as his first wife years before—so for all his years, he was now alone—and he feared he had been wrong all his life. They were always naughty boys, he and his brother, and part of that naughtiness was rebeling from what we taught them about the Savior. Their friends didn't believe, so they chose not to as well.

His eyes were opened to the truth of the Message, and we hugged and clung to each other. "I'm sorry, Mother," he said.

"Will you come and stay?" I asked him.

"No, but I'll seek out others at Bethsaida."

We had been glad to find each other after the estrangement of the years, and though we soon parted, a deep rift had been healed and a sadness for my long-lost-soul of a son was lifted from my heart. There had been a heavy burden of grief in my heart not just for the children who died, but also for the two who lived.

***

Paul had felt guilty and responsible for the deaths of both his wives, seeing as how they died bearing his children. Because of this he couldn't bear to remarry and watch a third woman he loved die. However, when he joined the community at Bethsaida he found among their number an older widow-woman who acted as his housekeeper and companion. As a result, he was no longer alone and indeed because of that and because of embracing the Message, he felt happier than he had all his life. When I, Paulinne, met the reincarnated Paul in my present life in Manchester he was recently divorced and was once again lonely. The pull was that the last time we met (in Capernaum when I was Mary), it had led to increased happiness and a new companion... subconsciously he was hoping to repeat the pattern! There was no attraction for me, as I hadn't been the companion, and he'd been the cause of a lot of heartache.

The first part of the regression session had provided the answers to both my mysteries—now I knew why I had two names, and why the incident in the dark room had haunted me, even when I was Paulinne two thousand years later. It was the raw emotional energy that had imprinted it. It began with fear, then led to the end of all the years of Mary's disappointment and grief over her sons. It was a pivotal moment in the life.

So—I had my personal answers, but I had not got to the treasure yet!

Chapter 11
A Miracle

MARY'S Story Continued

The regression session continued, and more information poured forth as I continued to answer Veronica's questions and access Mary's memories.

One particular event had really blessed Mary's life, and it proved her most treasured memory. When she sat beneath the trees and reminisced, she would hug herself with delight when she recalled this. This is what happened.

***

Over the years there had always been those who said they'd seen the Savior since he departed the world. They said he had been back, and that when he came he did more teaching, and they recorded it, and then they shared it with us in the letters that we send round from community to community. Although this sounds strange, the words were always so beautiful that they made us even happier when we heard them.

You never know when or where the Savior will appear.

From what is said he never looks any older, and the proof is in the words he leaves behind. It's groups he appears to—so there are always many witnesses to the event, and they can't all be making it up—and he always leaves something beautiful behind—words, thoughts, teachings. One minute he's there, and then he's gone. He says he's pleased with us, because we're keeping the faith of the Message and doing what we should be doing—taking it out into the world further and further. It's a big task but it will be done, piece by piece. Imagine how it would be such a different world if everyone knew about the Message and the Good News and *believed it*. But we do our part, and you can't do more than that.

But I never thought to experience the Savior for myself.

It happened at one of our feasts of celebration.

We were all very happy, sitting, eating, and rejoicing. There were a lot of us there, all Children of the Message. I was only thirty-five then and my husband was still with me. I was sitting by Ben when ... Oooooooh! The Savior is here.

He just appears, and there is a complete hush, and he says, "Don't stop, carry on." Everybody is just astounded. Children get shy and hide under their mothers' skirts. Someone offers him wine and food, and he says, "Thank you."

But I didn't see him eat or drink.

It was astounding and he was just looking at us. He had such expressive eyes, and somehow you're receiving a message from his eyes as they look at you. He's doing that to all of us, even the little children peeping out from their mothers' skirts. Everyone is very quiet and we're getting this message, "Peace be still. I bring you good tidings. I want to share the joy in my heart, and I want to show you all that those things are real, the things you have faith in, the things that you treasure. I was among you, and I will be among you again. You're always in my thoughts and in my heart. All the Children of the Message will always be in my heart. Know that whatever happens in the world nobody can take that from you. That is a divine certainty. Go on loving each other and being joyful. Go on being happy in the father's gift."[42]

Then we're told to carry on with the feast, and he walks round, touching people, embracing everybody, holding their hands, giving a hug. He feels real, he feels warm, as alive as you or I. I touch his hair and it is real. There's no sign of any wounds. His hands are whole. His feet are spotless. He has not aged. He is radiant and well and has such a beautiful feeling of peace around him, and as he touches you he transmits this. We all feel like we're being blessed by his touch.

He says he's come because of our faith.

Because we love him so much it makes it easy for him to come, and it's a reward for keeping the faith.[43]

---

42 By which he means the gift that is your life.

43 The collective energy of our thoughts, feelings, and longing for him had made a bridge by which he could cross into our world.

There'll be a time he will be in the world, then there'll be a time that he won't be in the world. We're in the time he can still visit and still come. He says this is the second part of his ministry, nourishing the Church of the Message he left behind, helping people keep the faith, because it's like a candle that could so easily blow out in the cold winds of the world. And this is why his heavenly father is allowing him to do this, because it's necessary.

We all feel very blessed and that we've been given this great treasure.

He goes round and then somehow he's gone. We don't see him go— like we didn't see him come, and we're all pinching ourselves—did we imagine it? No, we didn't. Did you see that? Did you feel that? Yes. We don't feel like eating anymore or drinking. We're just so happy, astounded, speechless with astonishment. We gather round and hug together in a circle. We're affirming what happened, trying to make it real in the world by creating this circle.

We all take an oath and swear we will not forget and that we will share, and we will talk about it—of course being prudent as to who, when, and where we share it. But it needs to be remembered and shared.[44]

It was so otherworldly that even when it finished we were going, "Did we imagine that?" But yet I touched his hair, and he was real, and he held my hands and he put his arms round each of us, and it was really real when it was happening. But when he went...

But I did touch his hair, his hands, saw all his wounds healed.

It got less and less real as time went on because there was a strange dreamlike quality to it. It was almost as if time had stopped when he appeared. He just looked at us all eye to eye, and we stopped eating and drinking and it was like time stopped. Like it was a break in time—we had the experience—and then time started again. We knew it was real but we doubted the reality. It was like a waking dream, but it was more than that... It was strange, but something truly amazing had happened. It was a miracle.[45]

---

44 Try recreating this in your meditations and prayers, picture yourself in the scene, and tap into and touch a kind of magic that lies there—incredible peace and blessing and love.

45 I have a dawning awareness that when Jesus fasted for forty days and forty nights alone in the desert he communed with God and was shown events in the future—and that he may have bi-located through time. (If you read *Autobiography of a Yogi*, by Paramahansa Yogananda, you will see that amazing things can be done by a great soul; Jesus was a great soul.)

Veronica asks me about healing.

Yes, I did experience healing—I called for healers to help my children when they were sick, and of course healing may bring about a lessening of the pain, or a speeding up of the passing to the heavenly father, but it doesn't necessarily mean the ailing one will arise from the sickbed cured. Also I witnessed the speaking in tongues and saw flames of fire on the crowns of people at our gatherings.[46]

It's at our gatherings that healing takes place.[47]

One of us will have offered their home for the purpose, and we rearrange the furniture so that the room we are using is cleared, except for some seating pushed back around the walls.

When we've all arrived, and are gathered, we hold hands in a circle and we lift our hands up and pray. We invite the Savior in, and there's often about twenty of us together in the room. We ask him to be with us, and ask the Holy Spirit to be with us. We welcome in angels too, so there are unseen children of the holy, heavenly father with us as well. They help the whole experience of the gathering to intensify, help it to manifest.

We put our hands down and then we sit on the floor.

There's a letter read out, containing news from people we know in the little towns nearby, then there's a thought from the teachings— something the Savior said, and we think about the words, and people get moved to speak, inspired by the Holy Spirit, so suddenly somebody may put their hand up, or just say the things that come through them— sometimes beautiful new teachings, perhaps a comment on the teaching we were thinking about, like an addition to it. That might happen at several points in the circle, people throwing in a contribution.

Occasions when Jesus was seen bearing the wounds of the crucifixion could only have taken place after the resurrection. The apostle we know as Doubting Thomas only believed it was Jesus after putting his hand in the wound in Jesus's side. (The Holy Bible, revised edition, John 20:19–29.)

His forty-day fast is remembered by Christians even today in the observance of Lent, the forty-day period before Easter each year. (Easter is the time Christians remember the crucifixion and the resurrection.)

46 Kundalini fire, spirit fire, not physical fire. Probably visible because we were in altered states of consciousness with the heightened energy within the gathering.

47 A gathering is the nearest thing to a church service that happened in the early Church.

We're all listening, with our eyes closed, and thinking of the words and the feeling, opening our hearts and our minds, and it's a nice feeling.

When that's finished it's time to do healing.

So we stand, still in the circle, and turn, putting our hands on the shoulders of the one in front, and say,

May the light of the father be with you,

May the light of the father flow through you,

May the light of the father bring comfort and ease.

***

And we feel peace, sometimes heat, and then the circle breaks up for more informal activities.

Chairs, stools, or benches line the walls of the room.

People in need of healing sit on a stool, or whatever, and the sitting down is a signal that they have a need. The group has broken up, so two or three of us will go over and put our hands on the one sitting down, perhaps on their shoulders, legs, or head. We just pray silently, or sometimes we are given words to say to them.

It's just very simple.

Occasionally dramatic things happen—people may gasp or shake or shudder, even throw themselves on the floor, and if that happens you know there's some bad energy about to be expelled, so everybody comes round to help. We call out,

In the name of God, in the name of Jesus, leave this servant of God.

***

That's the command, and energies do get expelled. We call on angels to take the energies back to God.

During this part of the proceedings sometimes people speak in tongues, sometimes there's discernment of spirits—one going up to another and saying, for example, "Your mother is with me now and she wants you to know…" And the mother will be dead, but the angels have brought her spirit in to us. It may be a message of comfort that's given, but this part of the gathering is unstructured activity, and the gifts of the spirit manifest as they will.

We know we are safe and that nothing is a problem and that the angels are with us—and there's a feeling that the Savior is with us too, a feeling of presence and love—**and that's why we hold the gatherings because we get hungry for that feeling of presence and love, and that sharing**. It is food for the spirit, and it keeps us going. So we hold the gatherings quite often, usually once a week, and very often on the Jewish holy day because it is quiet then—but sometimes more frequently than that, say, if there is a special occasion.[48] It's always a quiet day because people are not working, so it's a sensible choice—although Jesus wouldn't mind what day.

Afterward, we have a drink. Water, sometimes wine, or watered wine, is passed round. We share it, and we have a communion among ourselves. We break bread, and the cup or goblet of watered wine is blessed before it gets passed round and round until it is empty; we take little sips and pass it on. It's **the water of life, the water of eternal life** we pass round, because it's been blessed, blessed to bring us eternal life. The bread is sustenance for the soul and the body, just as Jesus's words are—**the bread is to symbolize the words of his teaching**.[49]

We give each other a hug and a blessing for the journey home, and we go.

Sometimes we go in twos and threes, and chat on the way home, or a group of ladies may go together and drop off at each other's houses. Or we may go home and share a meal and talk about what happened at the gathering.

It is very simple, very joyful. It's like our life blood—meeting and keeping the faith alive; keeping in touch with each other, and in touch with the living Christ, and keeping the Christ living within our hearts, within us as a community.[50]

---

48 The Jewish holy day, the Sabbath, falls on a Saturday.

49 **Mary's comment on how the communion is done today was, "There's no talk about it being his blood and body, that's morbid. We wouldn't do that. We celebrate his life not his death."**

50 Christ is a title for Jesus, meaning the Messiah.

Veronica asks about the letters we read out at the gatherings.

Letters are very important for us.

We get together and read them, to share news and comfort each other, and support each other, and to help each other. We share human news and we remind ourselves of the Good News, perhaps with a special thought to think on, to bring us more joy. It is good to keep in touch, it keeps us safe, and this is how I knew where to go when I left Bethesda.

There's always someone at a gathering who can read the letters out.

I can read, but not every letter is in the same language. I can't read Greek for instance, and there are Greeks and Romans among us too, so sometimes the letters are written in Greek. Then we call in a friend to read them, and the friend may like it so much they join us. We grow in number, and we attract more people this way, because it is such good news, such a lovely message about how things are, about the kind and loving God whose children we are. (And when I left Bethesda I was really looking forward to reading the letters that were at Capernaum. I was hoping they held some I hadn't read!)

But we don't just keep them, we send them on, and the letters go traveling.

Veronica asks who I mean by "we."

By "we" I mean the network of helpers, companions, and friends who keep the faith. We keep the Message alive that brings us so much joy, and that makes life worth living.

Veronica asks about the Message.

The Message says there's no need to have so much money, which is the thing that most people chase after. There's something else much more important that's inside us, that's completely free. The Message is the news of our heavenly father—and who we really are—what life is about. It's not about chasing coins and gold and money, it's about service, about love, about joy, and about enjoying the gift of the heavenly father—the beautiful home we inhabit, this world, and that we're here to do his work in this world, here to spread the Message, share the joy, and bring that freedom to other people so that they're not tied up in knots by the search for money. You have to have a bit of money, but it's only a means to an end. You only need to have enough to eat, live, and have a roof over your head, perhaps a donkey... some have a vineyard... but just enough to be comfortable in a small way. You can have more; some of us *are* rich and they help the ones in need. But money is not the focus of our life.

We treasure the letters and look after them. They get sent around, and sometimes the same one comes back! People write new ones... and one day they'll collect them all together and write a big one with them all in, because that has started happening.

We must not lose the words because they're so important. Little bits of paper in the world can get lost, stolen, damaged, burned—used for something completely inappropriate like lighting a fire. There are people who don't realize how precious they are. Like somebody's wife who's a bit impatient with it and doesn't want to know about the Message, and her husband has come home with this letter. She might just light the fire with it. There's a bit of wickedness as well out there! And people never like you knowing more than they do—especially those who can't read!

Veronica asks who is collecting the letters.

Younger people than I... men.

Men have a bit more power and a bit more say-so in our society, which isn't quite right, because we were all equal in the eyes of the Savior when he came. And we say "Savior" because he was the one who came to save us from the ignorance of not knowing. **It's the letters that hold his Message.** What people remember has been written down in the letters, to preserve it.

We People of the Message use the fish symbol because the Message is the food for eternal life, and you can eat fish. Some of the people who helped the Savior were fishermen, so it must have been one of them who first thought it up. Everyone knows what a fish symbol is. It only takes a couple of lines and a spot. Simple, you don't have to be good at drawing:

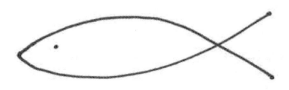

Food for the soul, food for the spirit, food for the heart, food for the mind—this is what the message is. This is what we have—spiritual food, as much as food for the body, because you need both; otherwise, you are not really alive, are you? You've got dead eyes, you're dead inside and you're just ticking off the days. Just plowing through the days, and that's no good at all, whereas you skip and dance through the days when you've got food for the spirit, **which is why the Savior came and brought us the Good News about how we are eternal and how we don't really die, because we just go back to the heavenly father, back to our Home.**

Veronica asks what the fish symbol was used for.

It's a bit of a secret sign between us.

If you see somebody with the fish, or they make the fish, they're saying they're one of us, because you do have to be a bit careful. There's a bit of trouble in the world, here and there. Not everybody likes us. We're a bit too irrepressible, too hard to control, too jolly, too open handed. There's a very mean spirit abroad in the world, and that mean spirit is the one that brings the tyrants and the controllers, the heavy taxes, the bad governance, the cruel yoke that lies very heavily on people. That's the mean spirit and that's nothing to do with the Message. We all help each other so nobody gets crushed. That doesn't make us popular with the authorities, because we take away their means of control. We're just too free. We have to hide our light because our light is too bright, so we do keep things secret.

We have to spread the Message, but we have to be prudent. We have to have secrecy, diplomacy, and perspicacity; we have to know where it's right and who is right to have it shared with, and the time has to be right. You can say the right things to the right person but at the wrong time—and they're not ready. We get help with that. We get discernment. We get whispers in our ear. The Savior said to listen to the words in our heart, to listen to the words of the angels, those unseen children of the heavenly father that are here with us. (Some people see them sometimes, but generally we don't see them—but that doesn't mean they're not there when we don't see them.) Angels are the helpers of the heavenly father. They bring messages and help His will unfold in our world.

People say they've seen them as figures robed in light, with wings. The Savior's mother saw one, and other people have. I haven't, but I'd love to see one. I've seen them in dreams, singing in dreams—a beautiful feeling. They say the Savior's mother saw one and that's how she knew her baby was special, or at least coming to do something special, and that she needed to take very good care of the child—which indeed she did, because he grew up and brought the Message. She was a lovely woman by all accounts, very kind, very well thought of. So was his father. I never heard a word said against him, and his other brothers and sisters were all nice people.[51]

Veronica asks if the Savior had many brothers and sisters.

Oh, yes, but they didn't have the Message. I think some of them were interested, but that was before my time. He was the first, the eldest. He liked his brothers and sisters, he loved the little children as they were growing up, from what I've heard. I've had a lifetime of hearing stories and reading the letters ...

Veronica asks for an angel to whisper one of the stories for the book.

That he didn't really die.

Not in the way you think of it, not in that final way, and because he didn't die in the same way as people, he can still come back because he isn't bound by the laws of the body like we are. Certainly, there was the enactment of the passion. But things aren't always quite what they seem. *(And there was more from the angel on this, but it will be better shared later in the chapter.)*

Veronica tells me to go to the next important event.

It is my last day.

I've been at Capernaum for two years now. I've been happy here and I've led a very simple life.

I'm in bed.

I'm preparing for sleep... Then I notice there are two angels at the bottom of my bed!

Oh! I've always wanted to see angels. And they are just like they say—there's a lot of light. I see wings, and beautiful white light raiment, and golden hair, and they are reaching out their arms to me.

---

51 Mary had visited Capernaum; the people there had actually met her. (Matt 12:46, 48, 49)

Haniel is to my left and Jophiel to my right. Oh... these were the angels I prayed to many times for my children...[52] I rise up out of my bed, but my body stays in the bed, and I rise up in my spiritual body. I reach out my hands and hold their hands. It's such a beautiful feeling, and they're taking me up and they're singing.

We go up through the roof and over the city.

I see the night sky and the stars and more angels, circles of angels all around the city, and we go up to them, up into the sky, and the Savior is there. Oh, I'm so thrilled. He's reaching out his arms and the angels are taking me to him. He encloses me in a big hug and somehow I melt into him and everything just melts, and then we're in a beautiful light.

We go to a heavenly garden—and there are my children! And my husband!... Even friends who've gone before me... I'm being welcomed. (It's been a lovely life, I've been welcomed everywhere! Even into the afterlife!) And there's so much love, and the love is like a vibration you exist in, like the floor under your feet is love—and it's all around you, and it's woven within you. It's just wonderful. We're reunited and they're pleased to be with me again. They're saying I'm going to be so happy, and they're so glad I'm with them. And I get a nice time here with them before I'm ready to go higher, into the realms of light.

This isn't the mansions of the heavenly father, this is a threshold.

I need to have my life assessed and have a life review. There will be angels and an accounting, and only then will I be going on to the mansions of the heavenly father to find a place where my spirit will be happy, where I can heal the wounds of incarnation.[53]

---

52 The two angels were embedded in the Jewish consciousness, so talk of them was not extraordinary. And these were two of the archangels that were also very active in the early Christian Church.

Haniel was very popular and very caring toward mothers and children. She was approachable and uniformly popular to beseech for mercy and the gift of a life restored. Jophiel was perceived as more male and powerful—so it was Haniel's mercy and Jophiel's power that was invoked to help the ailing one. Jophiel offered protection from the chill winds of the world's wickedness.

(When I tried to find out more about the angels afterward I found Haniel's name means *Beauty of God*, but Jophiel, whose name has many versions and widely differing spellings, means *Glory of God*, *Joy of God*, or *the Grace of God*. Jophiel is said to guard the Tree of Life for the Creator, and was given the task of banishing Adam and Eve from the Garden of Eden.)

53 At the accounting, you go back through your life looking at your choices and actions and you

And then you just bathe in this love and heal and you're back Home back with the divine parent, the heavenly father... **and there will come a time when you can be a messenger again, when you can carry a message in your heart**. Oh! But it's a rocky adventure sometimes when you come back.

Perhaps I'll have a longer stay this time.

***

Although this had been a happy life (and that type often don't need healing), at the end of the regression session I had to release grief for the children—because some of this energy was still lodged in my core. Guided by Veronica I chose to use a Diane Park technique I knew, and decided to make grief into an object. I visualized the heavy dark energy of the grief as a brick in my guts... which I then gave to the angels to take to Source to be recycled back into pure divine energy. I visualized the area rebalancing and healing with divine light.

That was the only healing we needed to do.

Basically, Mary had been a good woman who did her best and who lived a very simple life. She chose to experience thoughts of joy, gratitude, and love at every opportunity, but from time to time she had been overwhelmed by her grief.

But in the expanded state of awareness at the end of the session I was given an overview of the situation.

Jesus stopped manifesting to people before Mary died; it was something that happened just for a while. (All those with firsthand experience of him had died by then.) And shortly after Mary's lifetime there were lots of gospels, many more than the few we are familiar with now. (They are scattered, in old monasteries, some are held in the Vatican, and many were erased and written over in later centuries.)

We had the letters because people had written down what they remembered, and these we treasured.

---

experience what you caused others to feel. This may be intensely painful ... or joyous, depending on how that life was lived. And although there is a healing peace in the mansions of the heavenly father it is only in a general sense. We may have acquired scars on our soul that go so deep they need to be worked out in yet another life. We don't escape all our history, we just get strengthened to face it by the healing peace. (The scars and imprints on our soul are termed samskaras, which is an ancient Sanskrit word.)

'ords were only just beginning to come together.

was growing but it was also being threatened—but the
᠁ge was vibrant and alive, it brought a lot of joy—and that's how
we got converts. People saw the joy and wanted to know more.

The early Church knew about reincarnation. It made sense of Jesus's teachings.

1. He said life is the gift of the heavenly father, life is where you can express love.

2. When you do, you take that love with you, because it's your spiritual gold, and it's your gift to the heavenly father when you die.

3. And then you have a nice healing sleep in the mansions of the heavenly father, and when you're ready...

4. You come back and have another crack at things, and try to do even better in your next life.

The Bible doesn't mention reincarnation because some people removed the letters that had the teachings. And a lot of things changed when the Church passed out of our hands. It was in the hands of the true believers at this stage, the devotees who devoted their life to the truth and to the Message.

Then there came a point in the world when the Roman Empire thought Christianity could be a useful tool... and it did change. Total change set in. Consider the way we looked at money—because the Church became very greedy.

Christianity was then used to control people.

Basically, we'd annoyed the powers-that-be by being so free, and then they persecuted us, and when they finally decided *we won't fight it but we'll use it*, they changed it and we weren't free. They changed the emphasis, the cross became its symbol, and they took their scissors to the parchments. They had the power, the money, and the voice.

Some of it survived, but that's why this book is important because it is plugging a hole where some of the snipping took place. Jesus's appreciation of the value of women was snipped out too.

Women were held equal in the early Church—equal in every way: equal to administer the Message, equal to have their share of the gifts of the spirit, equal in the sight of the divine parent. Inequality was a big perversion that set in later, and reflected the overwhelming power of men in a patriarchal society.[54] (Women ministers are still controversial today, having been outlawed for the best part of two thousand years!)

There is very little mention of the devil and hell in the written texts of the Bible, but that was a huge part of the Church's teaching afterward— using fear rather than joy to control people. **We certainly weren't thinking of the devil and hell, but just of the joy of love.** And we weren't doing it to reserve a place in heaven. We already knew we had one—like we all do—we all get what we need after we die, which is why God/Home has many mansions.[55]

Jesus's Message was successful because it gave you so much joy— when you were living the days of the gift of the heavenly father, living the days of your life.

"Hellfire and brimstone" was pure control. It actually contradicted Jesus's message of the many mansions—where no matter how damaged and shriveled the soul, it will *eventually* be found somewhere, a healing home, in the reaches of the heavenly father. God doesn't have a sin bin. You just get what you need, and even the lessons when we stray into the dark side are valuable as part of the fruits of Creation. There isn't a wicked judgment that goes on, there is just an evaluating and then, "What is the necessary next step for this soul's evolution?"

---

54   Jesus lived in a very patriarchal society and he had to tailor the Message to the ears that were hearing it. The Jews he was preaching to expected God to be "He," because their priests had made God male in the scriptures in an attempt to legitimize men hogging power. Hence Jesus used the term "heavenly father" and not "heavenly mother," because no one would have heeded him otherwise. But God is father, God is mother, God is everything. If God really was only male He would be very incomplete. We really need a new pronoun for God … This overmasculinization of the Divine has unbalanced the archetype, and this is leading to trouble. Jews, Christians, and Muslims all call God "He," and think how much bloodshed there's been between them, and even between different sects of the same religion. This imbalance is likely to be the cause of another great wound in the time line (explained on the next page). Remember, Jesus was at pains to depict his version of God as a loving, caring parent, not a jealous and demanding God.

55   Like in Nadia's story of the miser. But this is not to say hell does not exist. It does. The devil and demons exist. The psychic, thought, and emotional energy humankind has invested in hell has made it a certainty that some will experience it, because we tend to get what we expect when first we die. (But the topic of darkness and light is better explored in *Holy Ice*, my next book.)

***

I've come to the bit I promised to share later in the chapter—the bit about Jesus dying.

Although the angel in the session was talking to Mary, some information came through that was for me, as Paulinne and not as Mary, so it did not actually belong in Mary's story. I was told that there were time lines where the crucifixion didn't happen, so there was a different outcome, and the Message was received in a more gracious and appreciative manner by the world at large. So we do have time lines where Jesus's words are alive in a better way than they are in this time line. But we've actually incarnated here to heal this time line, this particular time line that we're in has suffered an enormous wound with the crucifixion. It wasn't destined to happen but we're making the best of a bad job.

It wasn't quite as final as it looked because there are different levels of reality and we had to see cause and effect—and we had to see the result of the hard-heartedness, the political seeking, and the power play that ruins our world. This is why it happened, because people were abrogating their responsibility, like Pontius Pilate washing his hands of it, and there was jealousy, vindictiveness, and just plain wickedness. (We have to be prepared for the wickedness of the world, and if they could do that to Jesus what could they do to us? So we need to be circumspect and prudent.) It didn't actually stop anything and doesn't have to stop us. It's just a bitter lesson mankind needed to learn because we have such potential. We have a great potential to get it wrong and to get it right.

We have all incarnated here now to heal this very wounded time line, and by golly we better had, because that isn't the only wound there'll be in this time line if we don't. So this is why our life **now** is so important, and for us to understand the death and the passion properly and to honor the Message that the Savior brought is very, very important. It **is** the key to mankind's future.

In Guy Needler's book *The Origin Speaks* (chapter 10), he channeled material that implied the crucifixion was a kind of mass hypnotized event, and that although people saw Jesus dying on the cross it was an illusion. As you know, as Nadia I witnessed it. I saw Jesus on the cross, but when the light drained out of the world as he passed, it was not just clouds over the sun but more like an energy drain on reality. It was strange. Something happened, but it didn't happen quite like it looked, the angels were telling me in the session. They said, **we just need to know how precious the Message is and how important it is that we live it because that alone will heal the time line and prevent the further wound that's coming in the future if we don't.**

(We will have had teaching in our dream state, and we will have brought keys in with us into this incarnation to be activated by things we read and experience. The purpose of this book is to turn those keys, and by doing this to assist positive change in the greater world.)

So to sum it up:

- **The whole purpose of life is to express love**

- And to be kind to the other children of our divine parent

- **To garner as much love as we can**

- And to bring it to the divine parent when we die.

Contacting the Divine

After I meditated to see where I'd met Naomi's acquaintance before, I was given a simple visual key to contact God for answers.

"What follows is all thy doing," rang through my head, and I thought, "Oops, what have I done wrong now?" automatically thinking the worst! But I was rewarded with an enhanced communication with higher levels. It came down to a simple image that opened communication with my God-self.

First, relaxed and with my eyes closed, I had to picture a sea scene, with the sun high in the sky to the far right. Then I had to still the waves until the water received and held a perfect reflection of the sun to my far left. Then I had to cut through the water, as if it were a fish tank and I could look in through a transparent glass side. Then written in white light, words appeared against the backdrop of the dark water, or sometimes the words were spoken silently in my mind.

It always started the same way, with "Paulinne my child," and then it would go on with "Know it is the lord thy God speaking with thee in the dark worlds of form and matter..."

So first I was greeted, and then the communicator revealed their identity.

Beforehand I would have written down the questions I wanted to ask, and now with eyes not focused and half open I could ask and write down what came in reply. When I'm doing this my writing is loose and flowing but quite legible.

I find it works best if you are not emotionally involved with the outcome. You need a very calm emotional body to act as a mirror for you, if the communication is not to be distorted. So dreams work well, because they are only dreams and you are not attached to them. It's comparatively easy to remain neutral when receiving the words that will give you their meaning.

In the picture the sun stands for God, the sea is my emotional body (subject to storms and turbulence), and only when it is subdued can I receive guidance from above. (As the reflection is to the left and not straight in front of you, it means you are out of your body to see this, already in a higher state than normal.)[56]

So there you have it, it's very simple but with a little practice I have found it enormously helpful.

(I was told it will only work for those who need it. But keep hold of your common sense, because no human channel is 100 percent clear, and what we receive is vulnerable to being edited by our ego. That's why I use it for dream interpretation; there's less temptation for the ego to block, interfere, or embroider what is coming to you.)

---

56 In 2018, I found where this came from. Around fifteen hundred years ago, after the Romans left Britain, the land was governed by many Celtic kings. Rivalry was intense and they tended to fight each other—when they should have been united to repel the invading Saxons. Merlin, he of the legend of the time of King Arthur (for Arthur was one of the Celtic kings), saw the danger and embedded a network of spies in the courts of the kings so that he could unify and coordinate a response to the Saxon threat. I was trained as one of his spies. Communication via the inner worlds was one of the tools we used, and this image derived from Merlin's Celtic Druid background.

There will be more on this in *Holy Ice*, my second book, because this life of mine involved crystal skulls.

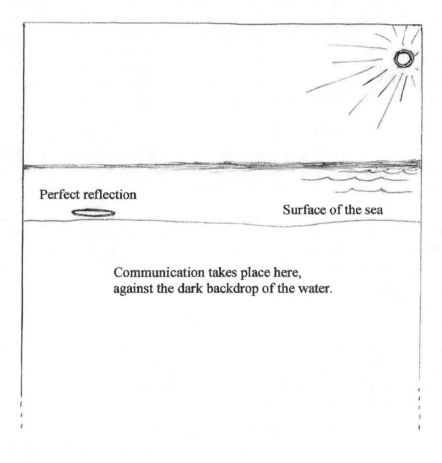

Perfect reflection

Surface of the sea

Communication takes place here,
against the dark backdrop of the water.

My Humbling Meditation Experience!

Around the time I was given the visual key, I had an experience that left me in no doubt about my lowly status in a spiritual sense.

I was meditating as usual, when I felt myself rising up out of my body. Up and up, until I was peering through the ankles of angels. Circles upon circles of angels were worshipping and praising God.[57] I was so far from God that I could catch no glimpse at all, but I tried and tried to see more through the gaps around the angels' ankles. I felt very small compared to the majestic angels. Then I felt a wonderful sense of bliss and peace emanating from God. It was streaming through the circles of angels. It was lovely, all thoughts and cares dissipated, just fell away, as I luxuriated in this heavenly bliss.

But I could not stand it for long.

Very soon what had been bliss ceased to be comfortable. The darkness within me was stirring and I had to get away. I just couldn't take any more bliss! And I returned to my body feeling very humble, after a **very** short time.

Oh yes, I've got a long way to go before I will feel comfortable there, even in the outermost circle of the presence of God. Always worth remembering!

Walk-Ins

The turn-around between Nadia dying and Mary's life was tight. There was only a brief visit to the mansions of the heavenly father, and to save even more time I did not incarnate in the usual way. I walked into Mary at twelve, just before the teaching began.

There had been an accident. Mary had been knocked unconscious by a runaway cart. No bones were broken, but in the unconscious state my spirit came in and the original one left—we swapped over. She had been a caretaker for the body of Mary and had volunteered to do that because she owed me a favor. It was a karmic trade-off. This meant that I came into the life at the point where Mary was introduced to the Message, but as I had access to the body's memories there was

---

57 By God, I mean just my God-self, not Source. Source gives rise to everyone's God-selves (see Figures 2 and 3 on pages 36 and 37 in chapter 2).

a complete continuity. (Like when you wake up in the morning and slowly connect with your memories of what you were planning to do today.)

The walk-in situation is not as unusual as you might think, and a typical point where this happens is during a period of lost consciousness, like an accident.[58] When Mary recovered consciousness after the nasty bump on her head—and I was now Mary—I'd experienced the usual forgetting that happens when we leave the spiritual world, and I'd latched onto the brain's memories and assumed they were mine.

The regression spontaneously began when Mary was already old, and in the session we didn't go back further than when she was twelve. I had no idea about her walk-in status then. It was only when I was looking for answers about time in a later meditation that I found out. Apparently there had been no need for me to experience Mary's childhood, because it was her time in the Church my soul was craving for—so the walk-in situation offered the opportunity to finish Nadia's life and still catch the very early Church that Mary experienced. And I was told,

Time is a tool for the heavenly father to achieve His purpose.

It furthers His aims, brings things into form and flow.

But time is not as we know it in the limited functioning of Earth.

So of course, it didn't end there.

---

58 In Needler's *The Origin Speaks*, chapter 18 is about walk-ins if you want to know more.

Chapter 12
Other Children of the Creator

The heavens are filled with stars, myriads upon myriads of suns beaming out their light into space. Countless worlds orbit the suns... Can this really be the only little dust mote in the universe where consciousness woke up to become aware of itself?

And are we the only ones deserving a helping hand in our spiritual evolution?

***

I still hungered to know more of Jesus. There was more, I knew; I dimly remembered a session I'd done in Manchester years earlier as I searched for the world with pink skies, where everything was easy and simple (the pink skies mentioned in chapter 6). And as I looked at more and more of my past lives I'd discovered I was a wanderer— that I had incarnated up and down the spectrum of dimensions, and wandered from world to world, as if I were no more than a dandelion seed drifting through time and space—although more often than not I did return to Earth at the 3D level, which is where we are now. I have lived lives beyond the counting on Earth, and I have a heart link with Earth.

But to recapture and explore the information held in the life lived under pink skies, I needed to arrange another regression session with Veronica.

We agreed on a time, and on a lovely spring morning in April 2016, once more I prepared to enter the inner world.

As I neared the point on the inner journey where past life memories are accessed, I found a wooden door. It was set within a wooden door frame. The door was well polished, old fashioned, solid, and reliable. "A door you can trust" were the exact words that came to me. It had a brass knob and panels. There was something comforting about that door, and I knew it would take me to the right place.

I open it.

I step through.

I find I'm in a pearly-gray light.

I'm traveling through the pearly-gray light in my body. I do have a body... but it's not human. There's a clunk... **I've just arrived somewhere.** My body—that is the form I inhabit—is my adult form.

When I travel I float into the pearly-gray light, and I re-coalesce when I arrive at my destination—and that was the clunk. It means I've arrived.[59] For short distances we simply walk, but we use this technique to move about on our world's surface from point to point.

Veronica asks if we leave our world.

That would be too difficult.

Our atmosphere is very dense and opaque, we see only faint glimmerings of stars, so we don't think about them much, and we've never looked beyond our atmosphere. We've never thought about other worlds. We're very much surface dwellers; we just hop about like this to different points on the surface when we need to get together for meetings.

There are a lot of us.

When we need to pool our knowledge, or need to be told things, then we get together for an information exchange. Either we're interfacing with the information, to exchange it with each other or we're being given the information from a primal source.

Veronica asks about the primal source.

The primal source is our ruler.

The Mother of the People.

Our Queen. (And here I see an image of an enormous insect-type being. But when I glance down at my own body I realize we look like little ones of her.)

---

59 Traveling this way is like jumping through a hoop and landing with a clunk and a shudder.

Veronica asks me about my appearance.

We have wings that are very thin and transparent. The vibration of our beating wings is what takes us into the pearly light. We speed up our vibration so fast with our wings beating that we move into the pearly light, and then we stop and coalesce—and then we're back in reality, and out of the state of transition. (We dimension hop, up into the one above, and then drop back down into our own at the place of our intention—wherever it was we wanted to go.)

We have six legs. I'm standing on two now. I've a pair of legs holding something, and my middle pair (around my wing area) are folded.

I am insect-like.

But I am a biped really. The main legs are the ones I'm standing on, and the other legs are like hands. The folded set is another pair of hands, but I'm not using them at the moment.

I'm holding a cylinder-shaped object, and that's where the records are. It's mine. I'm a record keeper. Many of us have these. You're given your cylinder when you're given your job, when you step up to fill the post that's been allocated to you. When it has been deemed you are a record keeper you are given this holder of records—and some are very old.

Veronica asks what the records are about.

About us, about hatchings.

We don't so much have names as numbers, the number of your hatching, and the number you are within that brood. We have a resonance, a vibration, our own personal key vibration we bring in with us that reflects our talents from before. Each life we've lived is a note in the song of our lives, and when we hatch another is added. The last note is our name now. Numbers and names are just a vibration.

I'm from hatching 330 of this present queen, within my hatching I'm twenty-nine, so I was twenty-ninth to wake up and come out of the egg. There's always someone waiting as we hatch who tells us and sets the vibration—and then we answer to that until we die. A record keeper is always present when there's a hatching...

I have an iridescent body.

I have iridescent fine gossamer wings and iridescent fine scales on my body. If I turn the scales one way I almost disappear. The way they reflect light, I can almost make myself disappear by adjusting the angle of the scales. They cover my legs and body.

For traveling, when I'm beating my wings and raising my vibration, I adjust the scales and then I do disappear, I literally space-hop, I make a location displacement.

Veronica questions me about my location.

(Initially the being is stumped by the question—but my "Paulinne consciousness" cuts in to assess things, and I find myself saying on Venus, but not 3D Venus, not the Venus you see in Paulinne's dimensions—higher dimensions than that.) We're part of the swarms of Venus. We're not aware of other worlds because we can't really see them, the atmosphere here is very opaque. When we look up all we see is a pink mist with faint glimmerings through.

Veronica asks about the cylinders.

We make the record cylinders with thought. They're solid enough, we just think them into existence. We build with thought. It's all you need in these dimensions.

But something important has happened—and I've been called to a meeting. I'm at a meeting, that's why I was traveling in the pearly-gray light—it's a gathering of record keepers.

This happens periodically, when we're looking at who's hatched.

We have to give the new hatchlings their purpose. You can't have them just wandering about, they need a task, they need to be a something. So we scan their vibration and check through our records to find a match, and we see who has got the information on them, so we can allocate a fitting task—one they've done on a previous time they've been with us. This always happens. (And it's how we got our own jobs as record keepers. We've all been record keepers before.)

Most of it is routine… but this time there has been an anomaly.

There's one hatchling no one can find any records for.

There's talk about this happening in the past, when a being has come who's never been here before, but it *is* very unusual… And because there are no records on the hatchling, we're not sure what would be the best task to allocate it.

***

By the end of the meeting the consensus of opinion is to let this ride, let the being grow a little older and then quiz it on what it remembers—and then we'll find out. (Not finding the records could be simply a record fault, but perhaps it will remember being here, and what it did before.) We're just going to have to let the anomaly ride for a short while because they're only newly hatched, so they're not ready to do anything yet. They'll be off to the feederies, you might call them nurseries. They're off to be fed, to grow, until they're a useful size. At this stage we can afford to let it ride. But if we don't find a solution we can't have an idle and nonproductive member of our species.

***

I'm at another meeting.

The little hatchling is older now, ready to be given a job.

It is saying it hasn't been here before, that's why there's no record of it—*it knows it hasn't been here before because it has come to be here now*, expressly chosen to be here, for something new. It's a bit cheeky for a hatchling. It says more—that it knows why it has come—and it isn't to do one of the jobs we've got on offer! It's to do something different.

It's a very cheeky little hatchling indeed. It thinks it knows better than we do. We've been doing this job for a long time, and this cheeky little hatchling is saying it's going to change things!

That is cheeky.

It's come to change things, change what we know.

Well, we don't know quite what to do with it. We could just pulp it and send it for food—that's very tempting. We can't have things like this which shake the system, and we don't have passengers in our society. We have to be useful... *but it is quite charming*... this little hatchling, and that's why it hasn't been pulped... and it is very adamant. It is demanding to see our Queen. This meeting is to see if we're going to allow that to happen.

Two of us have actually been talking to it, and they seem quite convinced we should let it see the Queen. The Queen that lays the eggs is its mother—in fact, all our mothers. She is Queen of the entire colony.

So we agree.

We will try that.

We will take it to see its mother and she can decide. It's not our responsibility.

The two who have already interviewed it will take it, and they will tell us what's been decided.

But I'm curious, so I ask to go too.

No one else is bothered because it's just an annoyance, and the other record keepers all go back to what they normally do... because we like to be busy, that's our nature.

The three of us go.

It hasn't got wings yet, so we have to hold it. We gather round and hold it in some of our arms. We beat our wings—and swoosh—we're off into the pearly-gray, and then we arrive at the Queen.

It's warm here.

She's huge.

Our Queen is lying down resting, no egg laying today.

We're being beckoned. (We had arrived at her lower end and we go up to her head end.) She is looking at us wanting to know what brings us.

We say it's the hatchling. There's a problem with the hatchling—not a physical problem—not like it has to be killed because it's not formed right, no, there was nothing wrong with her egg. It's been a very good egg, we just don't know what to do now it's hatched. The Queen isn't at fault, no, we just need her wisdom. And this cheeky little hatchling has a huge energy field and it expands it until we're in it and the Queen is in it.

We don't have energy fields anything like this—it's huge.

There is some extra energy coming in.[60]

It's had a higher dimensional input, it's had its energy field stepped up to assist in this endeavor, and we're all in this massively expanded, charged energy field. The cheeky hatchling is conversing with the Queen—by telepathy—we don't use words. Thought is our tool for everything. But we can hear what is being communicated because we are in the same energy field, so we hear it too.

It is saying that we need to wake up as a species.

That we are asleep.

That we need to wake up to ourselves in a bigger picture.

It's time for things to change. Things have been going on for a long time and they are very successful but they are static.

We are part of a huge universe. We're one of many, many life streams—*so there's not just us!!!* Not just the swarms here! We have our Queen, but the Queen has a massive Queen, and this God-Queen made *all* the beings, not just here, but in the huge place called the universe.

There's worlds beyond counting, not just our world!!

And the idea is not that we stay still, we have to grow, not grow bigger, but grow in understanding of who we are, what we do. We have always known we're not just our bodies, because we have this thought-tool, this cylinder that holds the records of all our previous vibrations. But we didn't know we are eternal. We are being told that now. We just knew we reincarnated from time to time, that we could come back into another egg. But we are part of a very beautiful and huge pattern, and we are eternal, and we are offspring of the Divine Queen. The part of us that goes into our Queen's eggs is an offspring of the Divine Queen. The Divine Queen is pleased with us and with our Queen, but we need to grow and change and know more. The hatchling has come to introduce us to the Divine Queen.

That makes sense. How else would we know?

The Divine Queen has sent this energy that has expanded the hatchling's energy field (its aura)—and because of that we're being given pictures, and knowing, and information.

---

60 My "Paulinne consciousness" knew it was a boost of divine radiance, but my insect-self did not. It was beyond its experience.

We get a hazy view of the Divine Queen, we don't see Her properly... a hazy, silvery fire-like Queen a long way away... and from Her streams out all this energy, it makes worlds, and on the worlds there's life like us, and different sorts of life too, but all are children of the Divine Queen. She wants Her children to do well and be happy, to grow and learn, and then to come back to Her and bring their understanding so that she can learn from them... and She will be happy to see us, Her children, when we come back to Her! (Normally we just die and hang about here out-of-body until we incarnated by going into a new egg.)

We're part of a great big family we didn't know about!

We thought we only had our Queen and that was it.

Ooh, will we meet some of the other children? ...Not necessarily, no, but we needed to know we weren't alone and that there wasn't just our species—*and in fact when we die we don't have to come back here*—we can go into that greater world called the universe, and we can have our lives elsewhere, as different types of children of the Divine Queen.[61]

It's like opening a door for the record keepers—we need to know that beings will be coming here from elsewhere, and that this is going to start happening more and more now (the anomalies will be much more frequent), there will be beings coming here bringing new skills, so we'll be learning from them, and we mustn't pulp them. We need to listen to them and make new jobs, and from those new jobs we will learn things, and that will change us and help us, and make us grow as a species—and we can go elsewhere too, and take the good things we've got here and help other children of the Divine Queen elsewhere. Ooooh, we're part of a big family and we're being welcomed, and there's going to be lots of interchange. We have got as far as we can in our seclusion, and now we're being welcomed into the big family—that's why the cheeky little hatchling came. The cheeky little hatchling is a very favorite child of the big Divine Queen, it really loves that cheeky little hatchling.

We are allowed to feel how much love it has for it.

It is really loved.

We are very lucky to have it.

---

61 Being a wanderer I had already done that, but it was not normal, and because of the forgetting that accompanies incarnation I never remembered when I was here.

Our Queen is so moved.[62]

How moving it is to feel the love of the big Divine Queen[63]... And it's very exciting—things are going to open up and change, and we're going to learn an awful lot more that's new. We are very lucky the little hatchling has come, and very lucky we took due process and didn't just pulp it, and did actually consult the Queen and listen to the little hatchling. It would have been easier, but, no, this is right. This is a very good thing.

The little hatchling is giving us a blessing, especially for the Queen, for being a good servant of the Divine Queen and producing all her eggs and hatchlings, and for fulfilling her purpose well.

You can't fault our Queen. She's really wonderful and we owe her everything. She's not the only one we've had, but she's the present one. (There comes a time she is replaced, a time she produces special eggs out of which will come a new Queen. But she's not old yet—she's in her maturity.)

We have been very blessed here.

It's only because I was curious that I came, because I hadn't been changed. (The two who brought the hatchling had been exposed to its energy and had had a dose of it, they had been changed enough to know it needed to be taken to our Queen.) But I was just curious... Or perhaps there was some deeper knowing I had? An intuition?... Now I'm wondering if I've met the hatchling before. I have been here before, because that's how they knew I was a record keeper... But I've been somewhere else too ... I don't always come here... Memories are stirring... I know about that bigger world! Yes, I do!

I'm just being reminded.

I sometimes come here when I want a bit of peace. This is a very ordered and stable society. Venus is a nurturing place. I come when I need a bit of nurturing from a good Queen, when my soul has been a bit frazzled. I don't leave such a long gap that they've lost my records,

---

62 In human terms it's like she's wiping away tears. We don't have tears.

63 You can see how the gender of God is not absolute, but is always a product of the society that is coming to God. It was necessary here for the feminine side of the Creator to be at the fore. But when the hatchling was Jesus, for that's who it was, he tailored his Message to suit the patriarchal society he preached in, and then God was referred to as "He." It was just expedient in both cases. God is not limited to just being a "He" or a "She." God has no limits.

but I certainly don't come here all the time. Yes, it's right, there are a lot of worlds! The hatchling is restoring my memories. I'd no idea when I was just me, when I was just 330:29.[64]

***

So he is allowed to do the thing he came to do.

The Queen is asking him what we should call it in the records. What is the line of the task he's come here for?

And he says it is to change us, to be a catalyst. *To save us from being stuck in the old way of being that wasn't going anywhere.*

So we're going to be opened up now to a lot of new experiences. We could call him World Savior, or World Catalyst, or Opener of Eyes to the Universe, or the Bridge to the Divine Queen... And there may well be others coming too! He is very, very beloved of the Divine Queen, but She has other special children that She sends out like this, so there may well be more coming. It's worth keeping it as a permanent record of employment.[65]

He is going to have to travel around.

The two record keepers have been appointed guides, and they will travel in a group, and he's going to go round and visit all of us, and give us this experience, this divine infusion of energy and understanding. He

---

64 After being Mary, the guides and angels had popped me back for one of these Venus lives, so I could witness the being we knew as Jesus visiting other children of the Creator. His ministry did not stop just because he left us.

In the session I realized I have been on other levels of Venus, in different life-forms as well. Venus is a sort of second home for me. I love Earth, I love Venus. I've been in all sorts of places on all sorts of worlds, but I've got a back catalogue of incarnations on Venus and on Earth, considerably more than in most places. Certainly at this point in the span of my incarnations these two are hotspots for me to come back to. And it's a good recuperation place, Venus. Not in the 3D level obviously, that's ruined now. (But even when the sun has turned into a red giant and Earth is a cinder, there will still be life-forms on Earth in higher dimensions; the sun is thronged with angels now, and so will Earth be then. We will be the angels—or very like the angels, *but different, because we chose the difficult free-will route for spiritual evolution.*)

Having this life meant I could be with Jesus again, and even though it was so very different, it let me feel that wonderful feeling of divine love in the audience with the Queen.

65 On Earth we have had a few, depending on what the need is.

135

hasn't come to be here long, but long enough to visit us all and share this understanding.

That's fair enough. So he's got a job to do and the two record keepers who brought him are going to assist. I'm just very lucky my curiosity brought me and I had the initial experience with our Queen.

I can join the two record keepers and go with him!

I do.

We do that relocation traveling, to visit all the children of our Queen.

And when he's done that, it will be time to go; so there's a lot of going into the pearly-gray and crystallizing out of it, then telling whomever we're with, and then moving on. We do that till it's all happened.

"Now that you all know, there's no need to stay."

He says it is time to go.

We're all very excited at the thought of beings coming here from elsewhere, and us going elsewhere, and things opening up. We're quite curious about the universe now. So we all want to say "thank you" to him for coming and being brave, because he could have been pulped.

Word goes out and we gather.

The Queen and all her children are here.

He is here with the two record keepers. He has got wings now and he can go into the pearly-gray himself.

So we're all out on the surface of our world, in a warm, misty orange-pink glow—that's our atmosphere.

He just rises up and we can all see him. A big beam of light comes down. He is in the light and he's rising up and we're all being given a blessing, and we're touched by the light and we all hear,

> *Behold my child with whom I am well pleased.*

> *And you are my children with whom I am well pleased,*

> *And whom I will be welcoming into my realm.*[66]

---

66 These were the exact spontaneous words on the tape in the session. They have a similar ring

We will have a bigger journey after death; our reincarnation cycle has been stretched, expanded, and changed. That is how we will get to go into other worlds and how others will come here. So we'll grow, and learn more, and be welcomed by the Divine Queen.[67]

It sounds exciting.

There's a great feeling of happiness and that everything will be well, like we've passed a test. We've reached a point in our evolution where we were ready to cross a threshold and move on, and we have!

It's a formal opening of the door so we can cross a threshold.

And then he's gone.

The record keepers are going, "There'll be lots more jobs, lots of different types of employment. It's going to be very exciting tracking people now."

We all understand that changes are coming, and they will be good. We all sing, by vibrating our wings and rubbing our legs.[68] There's a huge emitting of happy and joyous sounds as we celebrate. And we all come together, and we all go round our Queen, and we're all celebrating. Then we go to sleep. When we wake up we go back to our jobs, but we're very happy, happy with much more open minds about change, and about what new experiences might be coming. It's like a big door has opened and a huge breath of fresh air has come into our world.

A gentle wind of change is going to be blowing through and bringing good things.

***

---

to God's endorsement of Jesus shortly before the end of his ministry on Earth, Matthew 3:17 and 17:5.

67 I have come across this situation before, where a species has a short-circuit in its reincarnation process—for example, the beings known in UFO literature as the Greys. (They are the classic alien, with a spindly body and large, black, almond-shaped eyes.) I discovered that when they die they become craft-bound spirits waiting for a cloned body to inhabit. Their strangeness makes them terrifying to people who have come into contact with them, but they are sad little creatures really, who would be much better off for a trip to the Divine. But they are avoiding God because they are trying to avoid a species recall. They are very stuck and very, very old. They were flying about in crafts before there was human life on Earth. There will be more on them in *Divine Fire*, my third book.

68 Like Earth's crickets do.

In the expanded awareness of the session more information came through. I was still in the character of 330:29, but my "Paulinne consciousness" was pulling in further input. "Old me," "present me," and my soul level of being were all involved to an even greater extent now, as the perspective on 330:29's life widened out.

I realized that some of those beings are still there, still reincarnating there, and they're helping to spread the Message because sometimes the souls drafted in don't know as much as they do. It's a very big universe and the speed of spiritual evolution varies.

In some places it is very fast while in others it is almost static, or worse still—moving backward. That is when the Divine Queen sends in one of her special children as a catalyst. Since the Savior came we act as a teaching colony for some of the very backward types of beings—they get sent in, when there's a new hatching.[69]

Basically, the special children of the Divine Queen are dropped into a society on a world, like a crystal into a glass of substance, and that crystal causes the crystallization of all the substance in the glass. The special children are catalysts that cause all of the substance that's within the vessel to change, and that's what the cheeky little hatchling did on Venus, and that's what Jesus came to do on Earth.

Although the change is slow to happen on Earth, it was much quicker and more thorough on Venus. On Venus they had a different relationship with free will and evil, and that's why it was quicker and the change was less challenged. Earth is one of the most challenging spots you can incarnate on, which is why it is such a magnet, because souls like a challenge. And then you get stuck, trapped by your karma, because it is not as easy as you thought, and you come back and back... sometimes you're on the wrong track and you make matters worse. Well, that's Earth, and it will get there in the end.

You need to have some difficult schools...

There's so much variety across the universe. It puts our Jesus visitation in context and shows how special and precious it is when a saviour like that comes to a world. It shows what a long way we on Earth have got to go; it wasn't all hunky-dory here when he came, we didn't just get together, rejoice and see him go, did we? Instead we crucified him and put a tremendous wound in our time line. The year 2012 brought the

---

69 Sent in by guides and angels and other entities who oversee the unfolding of Creation.

change of an age, and there's so much uncertainty with what this next period of time will bring because the wound has not been healed. The violence, greed, and power lust that brought the wound are still here. In fact, those factors are at work on a bigger scale, and the stakes are even higher now. We're on the point of a second wound, and it's to help prevent this that the book is being written—and of course it's not just me trying to prevent it. But the focus for all the spiritual work going on, all over planet Earth right now, is to try and ensure that we do have a future, and that we don't have a cataclysmic wound, one that could render Earth no longer viable as an evolutionary platform, no longer able to support life.

And if anything happened to Earth it would also affect Venus—and other worlds too.

You can't rip the heart out of a body and have the body stay alive, and the solar system is like a body where the organs are planets. Earth is its heart.

It was bad enough when Maldek was destroyed; all that remains of Maldek now is the asteroid belt between Mars and Jupiter. You can have a body and have your spleen removed, and your legs amputated, and it doesn't mean you die, but it's not good. But without your heart it's the end.

Veronica asks about the wound in the time line—how does it affect us now?

It's linked to all the wars and bloodshed going on; there are wars in lots of countries now. It leads to the cheapening of human life. Life is seen as very disposable in certain quarters, held very cheap.

Veronica tells me to go to a library in the inner world to find out more. She asks which guides are with me.

Angels, and there's a sense of Jesus being with me, and my guides Frances and Hera are here too. But I've recently been told I'm coming up to a guide change, as Frances is planning to step back when *Spiritual Gold*, *Holy Ice*, and *Divine Fire* are finished. Since November 2015 a new guide has been observing my work and meditations, in preparation to take Frances's place. That's why Two Wolves Dancing, a Native American medicine man, is here with me too. Watching. He was my father in a life with the crystal skulls fifteen hundred years ago, which I've written about in *Holy Ice*; he is my link with America and my future.

In the library the guides help me to access more...

***

The forces of Greed are stalking the world, even more than they used to, boosting the sales of arms and making wars happen. They are trashing the physical fabric of our world, and the wound could escalate—especially if a nuclear side is involved. We've got global warming as a result of greed and stupidity, and this massive arsenal of weapons could obliterate us. A steady stream of poison and toxins flows into the world through the weapons—and it's just a mess, but it might be an even bigger mess.

It depends on how many people wake up in a spiritual sense, because we need to make a shift in our consciousness, we need to open our eyes and see, and understand in a deeper way the consequences of actions.

There needs to be an awful lot of people who go, "Not in my name" and "Stop the war," like they did trying to prevent England being dragged into the Iraq war. We need to find a new way, and even just doing it in your own silent prayers will help. There needs to be a change in the energy of the world to bring about a harmonious and peaceful future, because we're rolling down a slope of destruction, further and further toward the pit of oblivion—which is not what Jesus came to help us do. He came to help us evolve in a spiritual way, to have the future the heavenly father would like us to have, a future of love and joy and harmony, a future of valuing and enjoying life in the beautiful garden that is Earth.

The second wound would be a terrible conflagration. It's questionable as to whether we've already had World War 3, because some of the horrific fighting in the Middle East could well qualify for that. But there is a possibility of something worse and even bigger on the cards.

It would be much better if it didn't happen.

But we're very vulnerable in the next few years, until the middle of the century; *very vulnerable to things escalating out of control in a huge cloud of destruction.*

The forces of Chaos are stalking the world, seeking victims, preying on people, preying on their greed and fear. There are a lot of Dark Angels (fallen angels) that actually feed on death, so their manipulations are behind some of it.

Veronica asks what can we do as an individual?

We can bring peace into our lives. By having a harmonic where we live, by keeping a watch on our thoughts, and stopping those momentums of resentment and bitterness and anger which can be so addictive. We are in control of our minds—but often we just don't bother to control them. Try to keep your thoughts harmonious, appreciate the beauty of the moment, cultivate an attitude of gratitude even for the small things of life. Prayer, meditation, spiritual endeavors of any sort are always good, and try visualizing a wonderfully healthy planet that we share with thriving life-forms—the birds, fishes, animals, and plants.

Picturing things healthy and well will help to ground a future where that's true. And don't go buying hardwood timber from the rainforest, because a lot of it is smuggled out with false documentation and ends up rotting in our gardens as garden furniture, only to be discarded after a couple of years. Support friends of the Earth and Greenpeace, which is a way of helping in a physical manner. Even the very tiniest direct debit adds up, when a lot of people make them.

Your own prayers and thoughts can change the thought forms that are crusted round our planet. We urgently need to get rid of all those thought forms of brutality, fear, greed, and limitation, to let divine light and radiance shine forth, into our hearts and minds. We can all chip away at that.

Read my books! Just having a physical point in the world like a book, means you can lend it to people, you can see it, and seeing it you are sending an energy charge down the optic nerve into your brain, reminding yourself; you are keying into the thoughts and information that's in it, lifting your vibration, increasing your radiance—and you're helping divine energy flow down into this dark level.

Heed your dreams, and be a good citizen of the planet. Listen to what Jesus came to tell us, and try to manifest that in your life. Never mind in how small a way, it all helps. Even giving love to the world by admiring a sunset—it can be that simple. Listen to and appreciate bird song, and send a thought of thanks to the birds. Admire flowers and thank the forces of nature that brought them into being—the nature spirits and fairies, the maintenance entities that look after our world.

And don't forget the angels, ask the angels to help us. Good angels need to be asked because they know we have free will, and they respect that. Fallen angels have no such scruples. And remember prayers are never wasted and neither is thought energy. Thought energy was so strong on that other world that it created things, and it is strong enough here to create things—it creates great momentums of fear and hate. It can be very, very toxic, or healing, depending on how we qualify that thought, depending on what quality we give it. We are powerful enough to create and manifest a good future and powerful enough to create and manifest a complete disaster.

It's up to us.

Chapter 13
The Stars

The sadness, yearning, and love with which I have always looked at the stars made me wonder. Before I called *Spiritual Gold* finished, I grabbed at the chance to see if there was more—I'd only dealt with one life stream on Venus, and there must be others in higher dimensions there, not to mention elsewhere. There has to be a myriad of ways that spiritual evolution ripples out across the worlds.

I wanted to know more.

There is yeast in the dough that is the universe; the yeast makes it rise and evolve. It's the "yeast" that intrigues me. You could say Jesus is part of the "yeast."

I'd met him on Earth and on Venus, although in very different bodies each time.

I had been trying to tie up the ends of the book, and I'd had a day where it just would not happen. I had finished the previous chapter, and knew what the last would hold, but it wasn't quite right as it was, and the more I tried, the more it was like trying to force things. Had it been finished it would flow... that told me there *was* more, and that's why it wasn't ready to tie up.

On a restless night I meditated to see what I could find.

I sat down and made myself comfortable. Leaning back on a favorite sofa, I closed my eyes, relaxed, and let tension flow out of my spine.

I pictured the light of God above me, flowing down to me, and silently said, "Silver-fire sun of my being ray down the crystal curtain of light all around me."

Safe in the light, I asked the archangels to help: Michael for his protection, Uriel so everything perceived and subsequently written would be imbued with truth, Raphael so that what was perceived and later read would be healing, and Gabriel that everything be imbued with love.

And I asked that my guides meet with me.

I took my favorite route to the inner world (when I'm working on my own, that is), based on the journey in *The Inner Guide Meditation.*

I pictured a cave and entered. (This is my cave. It is always the same cave.)

As I go in, to my right there is a pool. Sunlight beams down through a gap in the rocks overhead and sparkles in the water. I visualize bathing there, and I wash away traces of the outer world. Renewed and refreshed I walk further into my cave. I notice the floor I'm walking over, and see crystals sparkling on the walls. On and on I go, until far ahead I see light. As I get nearer to the light there is an opening in the cave wall, to my left. I go up steps and pass through the opening.

I'm standing on a grassy bank. A valley stretches out below me and my guides are there, already waiting on the bank just outside the cave.

Jesus is there—and he tells me we are dancing through time together! (He means the way we keep meeting in life after life.) He's laughing and dancing! I've never seen him like that... Frances is there, with Hera, and my new guide, Two Wolves Dancing. Two Wolves has been joined by Silver Brother, a wolf. This wolf is a power animal of mine, and he's an exuberant character. He'd come racing through the cave to meet me on my way in.[70]

70 I first met both Two Wolves Dancing and Silver Brother in a meditation in November 2015, when the bombshell was dropped that Frances would be leaving. (This was in the time of waiting, OMP had my original manuscript, but it would be April 2016 before I heard back from them. Publishers get a lot of submissions and have a very long waiting list.) Frances had been with me since my school days, but would be leaving when the three books were complete. This is why I'd been introduced to Two Wolves Dancing, who would be observing until he took over as guide. When I last knew him, he had been my father in a Native American life. He had been the tribe's medicine man, in a life involving crystal skulls, which is written about in *Holy Ice*, my second book.

Silver Brother had been a wolf cub I'd rescued in another Native American life. I'd found him trapped under a fallen tree after a storm in Canada, when I was inspecting my traps. His mother had abandoned him and he grew up with me. We loved each other dearly in that lonely life long ago. He helped me hunt and we were a team. It was good to see him again.

I tell the guides what I'm looking for, and we all go up into the stars. We come to a doorway made of lines of light. I stand in front of the door and put my hand on the doorknob. I open it slowly.

I step through.

***

I am looking at a very bright scene. Very bright white light infuses the sky above me, and white sand shimmers below me in the glare. I'm looking down from a cave's entrance, but the rock at my side is so smooth that at first I think I am in a temple doorway. The entrance is pyramid shaped, but naturally formed.

I look at my body.

I am mineral—my body is a pyramid-shaped crystal. It is translucent in places, transparent in others, smooth sided and absorbs light. I'm here absorbing light until I have enough energy to move. An area beneath my base has the ability to ripple forward and will carry me slowly across the terrain. That is how I'll emerge from our gestation cave.

A friend joins me, comes from behind me. More are following.

We're leaving the cave.

We flow down from the entrance and cross the sand, seeking a patch of the dark rock that makes up our mountains and is the bedrock of our world. We are seeking a high place, drawn by the light; the light will be even stronger there. When we find one, we will settle. There is no water on the surface of our world or in our atmosphere. We don't need water, but there was some in the cave, and it has a function at the start of our life.[71]

We pass others of our kind already rooted in place.

We find a place of our own, and we will no longer move. Instead, the base area of our bodies dissolves the rock we are on, allowing us to form roots. We mix the atoms of rock with our own, and filaments grow from us that penetrate the tissue of the rock. We absorb evermore light, and as we do, we grow upward toward the light and downward into the bedrock of our planet.

71 Water is an intensely spiritual substance. On Earth we see and drink 3D water, but it has a counterpart in other dimensions. The counterparts are linked. In higher dimensions I've encountered it called "vital fluid," which it is—it's always good to drink water.

That is our job, to grow. We do it well.

We will do it until all the planet is covered in crystal, until crystal penetrates its heart to its core, grounding the light. We "sing," we vibrate in our happiness at being here, at absorbing the light. For in the light is the love of the Creator and it nurtures us.

For we rightly see who we are. We are the consciousness, the brain of our world. We are its sentience and we hum with the rhythm of the universe in a hymn of thanksgiving to our Lord God, the Divine, the Creator of all. We are happy beyond measure. No darkness clouds our world. We have never known the darkness freewill brings, for we simply complete our purpose the best, the most fulfilling way we can. What else is there to do? Nothing. We are at total peace, fulfilling our world's dream of evolution. For we grow and grow and hold evermore light. Our world is filling with light. Light is in its very tissues because of us. It will be a world of light, forming a necessary balance to dealings elsewhere in the cosmos. This we dimly understand because it comes as whispers in the light. The photons of light bring us messages and wisdom and joy, and we rejoice in the love of being, being part of the Plan, being able to assist our Creator and fulfill our destiny.

***

But there was more, for in the light my "Paulinne consciousness" had detected another voice… a voice I recognize as Jesus—bringing us comfort and wisdom and more joy… helping us to understand the Creator, to understand love and being.

We sang, vibrated, rooted, and grew to the light until we covered our world, until it all sang and every molecule was sentient and sang. The planet evolved, we were more obviously a part of it than we are on Earth, where we appear to be so separate. But we're not as separate here as we look (!) I was told.

It's kind of like Earth's brain is us—this thin, mobile, squishy-bodied skin of beings moving about loosely on the surface of the world! That's Earth's brain! That's us! Our brain is tucked away in our skull, but Earth is wearing hers on the outside! (Take us away from Earth and it's like putting a tissue culture in a petri dish in a lab. There's a limit to how far it can develop out of its proper context.)

At this stage I'd drawn the meaning from the experience, and now I understood how it related to Jesus. I was awed to see that the Creator's love poured forth with such ceaseless abandon, a hidden force in the light showering into the universe through countless suns. And I was awed by the extent of Jesus's unconditional love and support for the life it brought forth, in whatever form, however consciousness is expressed. Light and the love that it carries act like yeast in the universe...

I don't know what I'd expected, but I'd been given something very profound.

Food for thought.

But now it was time to return to the grassy bank.

Once there, I thank my guides and say goodbye.

I enter the cave on my own, and passing through, return to ordinary reality.

I thank the four archangels for their help.

***

Well, that was Sunday evening, July 3, 2016.

But what else was there to find?

I *had* to go further than I could on my own...

At short notice Ye promised to regress me. By now he was working for the NHS, the National Health Service in England, as a dramatherapist in a child and family department. He was always very busy, and when he wasn't at work he was occupied writing—novels and poetry; writing and making music are his passions and the way he unwinds from the stresses of his demanding work. But he promised to do a session for me at the weekend.

It would be good to do a Psycho-Regression session this time. It had been a long time since we worked together. I love the beauty and deep healing I find in my own way of working – and as you will remember – I trained him.

I looked forward to the weekend.

Chapter 14

An Angel at Your Table

JEREMIAH'S Story

Saturday arrives.

I test the recording equipment, and pour spring water into the lovely blue glass goblet Ye always uses during a session.[72] I burn incense and say a prayer in my healing sanctuary, as I always do in preparation for any regression work. The room is white, the translucent, thin, floor-length crushed velvet curtains are white, and the carpet is a warm sandy-gold, the color of our beach here in Whitley Bay. It's a grounding color, that sandy-gold. The fireplace hearth is banked up with real sand and studded with candles. Graceful, fresh green plants breathe life into the spacious room. Colored glass in the bay window is just visible through the partly drawn curtains—the motif is a sunrise, showering spangles of yellow, orange, and gold light into the room. The drawn curtains will moderate the light, making it easier to visualize; too bright and it's a distraction.

I light a candle in the golden angel candleholder, and all is ready.

Ye appears, and I am tucked up all warm and cosy on the therapy couch. The relaxing music we use for the start of the session is *el-Hadra*.[73]

We begin.

I close my eyes; it's my inner eye that will be working from now on, my third eye.

---

72 To keep him in a state of purification. We always drink water in a session—and it's especially important if you are releasing negative energies at the end as part of the healing.

73 There's information on *el-Hadra* in a footnote to chapter 6, page 54, footnote 28.

*Ye takes me through the relaxation and deep breathing, and when my body is blissfully tension-free I am told **to visualize myself in a beautiful place in nature.***

...I am in a meadow. I see buttercups, and there's red clover and long grass all around me. Bees hum and butterflies flutter, small blue ones, red admirals, and white ones... It's early summer here... there's white daisies too. The blue sky has small clouds, hinting at rain to come. There's a stream below me, and a high, hilly bit above me where trees are growing.

It is warm and sunny, and I lie down on a sloping bank in the meadow to absorb the beauty and the energy there.

Then I meet my guardian angel.

She's in front of me, farther down the slope. She's very... white, there's a lot of white light, and although I can't see her face clearly I sense she's smiling. I can see fair hair...

She's showing me a cave.

We're at the entrance. It's in red sandstone rock...

This is not my meditation cave—it has a higher roof and darker rock—and there's sand on the floor, signs of rain, the sand's showing patterns, like when water's flowed over it.

There's steps.

...I'm going to walk down the steps.

I get to the bottom... it's sandy here ... More wet sand.

I see the spirit of the cave. It's a wolf. It's Silver Brother!—who makes me laugh, because he says, "Eager to help, boss," and, "I'll make a good job of guarding the entrance to the inner world. Nothing will get past me!"

(I'm doing this session hoping to find another life with Jesus. He had said we'd danced through time together—so it must have been more than just the three steps I already knew about. I had to trust that my higher self had dusted off the appropriate file and got something ready. But I have to confess, there were times in this session when I wondered how on earth it was going to tie up. However, patience was rewarded and my higher self did not let me down—but I'm sure

you'll understand what I mean as the story unfolds.)

I float down through the cave bed, down into my body through my crown, and scan through my body to find the main area linked to another past life where I had contact with Jesus.

It's my throat... It looks dark... sort of black.

Ye asks what the main emotion is that's linked to the past life.

Agony... and **anger**... and **disbelief** are the words that come.

I'm told to look at my feet and to tell him what I see.

Sandals... I'm a man.

Ye asks what I'm wearing.

Just something simple, cloth wrapped round my hips... I've arm bracelets on both upper arms, and tattoos... I've big tattoos on my chest too, like spirals. The cloth is just homemade, coarse, handwoven—a khaki, beige, natural color... I've a beard and long, tangled, dark hair, and arm bracelets ...

Are they gold or silver?

Copper.

Across my back I've a quiver, with stone-tipped arrows.

Have you got a bow?

Yes, a small one, also in the quiver. I've got a staff. I'm holding this long, stout staff. It's got a stone blade... it's a spear, but I'm leaning on it like a staff.

Are you outside?

Yes... it's flat here, sandy... it's hot, that's why I've not got much on.

What is your name?

Jeremiah.

How old are you, Jeremiah?

Thirty-two.

Is anyone with you, or are you on your own?

On my own.

What are you doing?

Waiting and watching, waiting for somebody. There's dust on the horizon. I think that means somebody's coming, or something is happening over there... oh, it's a battle going on over there.

But you're not involved in it?

They are not my people, but I'm watching. I don't want trouble to come any closer. I've got a family, I've got people to protect. That's why I've brought my bow and spear. It gives me a bit of a view here. I can see what's happening. But there's no one near us.

You've got a family?

I have. I've got sons too young to fight, and daughters too, and a wife, Rebekkah. My first wife, Miriam, died. I've got the children from two women—five sons, all young, and three daughters. That's a lot of mouths to feed... but it will be good when they're grown—if they grow. They don't always live to become men... I'm worried, and I want to protect them, that's what's brought me here... I've walked a distance to come here, because I've heard what's happening.

Do you know who's fighting?

Medes and Persians. They're not my people.

Who are your people?

My tribe.

Does your tribe have a name?

We never think of ourselves like that, we're just us, and everybody else is an outsider. We're on the inside, we're in the tribe.[74]

Is there anything else you need to understand, or can you let this scene go?

I can let it go.

---

74 Possibly a tribe of Scythians, or Sakas as the Persians called them. They used short bows, and tattoos showed a man's standing in the tribe. A man without tattoos showed he was of low station.

Go forward in time to the next important event, and let a new picture come clear. Tell me what you see.

The fighting is still going on, and I've moved my family into a big cave. It's in a fairly desolate area, so I think we'll be safe. We brought what food we could with us, and we've killed some of the animals, so we are eating well at the moment, but I don't know how long we'll stay here.

Is it just you and your family?

Yes. The tribe dispersed. There are other caves, so we spread out. But it's inhospitable terrain, so we don't think we'll be followed here. We abandoned our village. Hopefully it won't be for too long. The children are a bit noisy, so if anyone did come up here they'd probably hear us, but we got branches and brushed our footsteps away as we walked, so there's no reason for them to think we'd be here, no reason to come up to the hills. It's barren land here, not where you'd grow crops.

Ye moves me forward.

I go back to see what's going on.

The dust has gone, the battle is lost or won—or perhaps it's just a retreat—but they've gone elsewhere, and I go to another cave to see if they've heard anything there.

Ye moves me forward.

They hadn't, but five of us, all men, go to look at our village to see if it's safe. We don't think anything came that near, but you never know with a battle—you can have stragglers running away in all directions, foraging, scrounging to keep alive, and then they burn things just so nobody can get anything if they were followed...

When we come to the village we find it's safe, nobody has come. Everything is alright. (We live in tents by a stream, and that's why we live here, because of the stream.) But just to check, we walk to another village to see what's happened there, but they don't know anymore than we do.

It must be safe to come back.

It's difficult getting water where we are in the cave.

We said we would send a signal to the others—a smoke signal—so we light a fire, and use a lot of green wood to send up billowing clouds of white smoke, so they can see it and know to come back. And then we go to meet them.

So you all go back to your village?

Yes, and life continues. It's not a bad life here. We grow a bit of grain, we have fruit, and nut trees, and we hunt.

Ye moves me on to the next important event.

My sons are older. They're from my first wife; they're eighteen, seventeen, sixteen, fifteen, and fourteen. My daughters are from my second wife; they're a bit younger, eleven, ten, and eight. I'm lucky to have so many, and they've all lived, so far...

It helps that we keep to ourselves, and so far no disease has come here. But you do hear tales of villages wiped out by diseases... And you can't keep completely to yourself, sometimes we meet travelers, and sometimes we go to markets where there are traders and lots of strangers—but basically we keep to ourselves. It's a very quiet life. Your biggest aspiration and hope is that your children grow up and actually live to become adults. You think it's a very worthwhile life if you can manage that.

You stay in the same place and don't move about?

We might move our tents up and down the stream, but we don't go far. You need water. This is a hot, dry land. It would be foolish to leave the stream. There's fish as well. There's no reason to go. We get on with the other villages around here. We are content. We don't need much as long as we've got food. It's just your family really, your family are your riches—the laughter you share and the love in their eyes. It's a kind climate, so we don't need much; it's easy to live out of doors here.

Ye moves me on to the next important event.

A trader has arrived.

He's got news. We don't have much wealth to trade for other things— so he's not going to be doing a brisk trade with us! But we can provide him with a meal...

The news is about a king dying—and then of course there's a new king. It doesn't really affect us... but there might be more fighting again. They're never satisfied are they, these kings? Always got their eyes on somebody else's land. He says to watch out because there are soldiers about again. And looking at my sons he says, "They'd like them. They'd soon get them kitted out and joined up."—So I'm warned, I need to be careful, or I'll lose my sons.

We get some little trinkets in exchange for the food, and we've given him food for his journey as well.

Ye asks if there's anything else I need to understand in that scene, or can I go on to the next important event?

I can go on.

Ye tells me to let a new picture come clear.

I'm back at the place where I was watching.

The place at the beginning?

Yes, watching to see if there are any soldiers. The trader said they were about...

I don't see any.

But when I get back, I discover the soldiers came the other way, and they took my sons with them.

All of them?

There's just my wife, who's very upset.

My sons said to her, "Don't worry, Mother, it'll be an adventure, and we'll come back."

So your sons weren't worried?

For all my telling them to be careful, they were looking for adventure. They wanted to be men. They were offered weapons. Oh my goodness...

She hid our daughters under a pile of cloths, and they were sensible and kept very quiet. You need your daughters to make marriage alliances, to make your tribe stronger, and you need your sons to defend it. But my sons have gone and all I have are my daughters—whom I love dearly—I should be thankful for small mercies—I've still got my wife. Because my sons went willingly they didn't do anything to my wife. It doesn't turn out so well if they, er, don't...

So what are you going to do?

I don't know what I can do. As the trader said, "You're safe, old man, they wouldn't want you now." (I laugh.) It's hard when you get older, and you haven't got the strength you had when you were younger. My hair's gray... but I'm still strong...

Well, if we stay here at least they'll know where to come back to. We will just have to pray for them and ask the gods to keep them safe. That's all we can do. It's an empty tent... My daughters hug me and say, "You've still got us, Dad."

...(I sigh.) They took our animals—I've lost my breeding stock. An army is always hungry, isn't it?

Breeding stock of?

Goats, a little herd of goats; they give us milk and cheese. We eat goats' meat and fish from the stream. And strangely enough I really miss my goats. They are very beautiful creatures, goats. I have big feelings of **loss, sadness, and grief**...

For your sons?

Mm... and the goats... They're as clever as people, cleverer than some... and unlike my sons, they didn't choose to go, and they'll never be coming back.

There was nothing else at this point, so Ye tells me to go to the next important event.

My sons come back! Not all of them. The youngest died—bad water or something. The others are battle-scarred.

They are all very jolly and full of camaraderie and tales of heroism and bravery. We sit around the fires at night and hear all their tales. They were paid—well, more like they stripped the bodies of the people they killed. They've come back with what you might call treasure. They say, "Dad, there's enough to buy you some goats. Stop going on about your goats!" They're promising to go to the market and get me some more goats. I should just be thankful they've come back, shouldn't I?

I do thank the gods, and I make a little offering. I shot a bird with an arrow and placed it on a special stone in our prayer place as a "thank you" to the gods, so I'm not going to eat that, but give it to the gods.

Four of your sons came back?

Yes. I was very lucky. I didn't think any of them would. You never know how far an army takes them. They can take them so far away they can't walk home.

They think it was a great adventure. The highlight of their life!

Sometimes you have to keep your fears to yourself, don't you? It just seems foolish to me to be killed in somebody else's quarrel, or because of some king's greed. Their advisers tell them to go to war, but it's not the advisers who are going to get killed.

Ye moves me forward to the next important event.

My daughters are getting married, all of them, at the same time. They're young women now, in their teens, and they are marrying brothers. That will be nice for them because they will be together... they're not far away either, a neighboring village, so we'll be able to go and see them. They are friends of mine, that family, the father is one of my friends.

They are very excited. They've got new outfits—their brothers dug up some of their treasure and did a trade for jewelry and for their bridal outfits. So some good things came out of that war.

It was sad that my son died, but it could have been much worse. I did get a couple of goats, and they've had kids now. We eat the boy goats and breed from the females. I want to build my flock back up, and at the wedding I'm granted loan of a billy goat.

(My sons are all married and they've got children... and it's not long before my girls give me more grandchildren—so that's really good.) Some of my sons live with me, some live in the other village where my daughters are.

My wife and I are happy. We've raised a lot of children and they've had children, so you can't ask more out of life than that. We've had enough to eat, well, more or less...

You must be quite old now?

Yes. My hair is white, and my wife—she's got gray hair. We still laugh. Life is simple, life is good. You just don't think about the difficulties, you just laugh and get by… and grandchildren, you can't put a price on that—seeing them playing, and scampering about, happy.

My sons have grown up into fine men, and they are treated with respect. There's nothing like a scar to stop people getting into a fight with you! (I laugh.)

There was nothing else I needed to see, my wife and I were content, and I go forward to the end of the life. I'm about late fifties or sixty, not what we think of as old, but I was just worn out. Ye asks if we are both still alive.

Yes, my wife is a bit younger than I am.

My sons have all come round, and my daughters too. I'm lying on my bed, skins, you know, goat skins and brushwood, and they're just saying good bye. They know it won't be long now. I'm holding their hands, one at a time. They kiss me on the cheek and thank me for being a good dad, and they say they won't forget me, and that they often think what I used to do with them, and that's what they do with their own children.

That's a nice thing to hear.

I was never harsh. There's nothing wrong with a smack but I never beat my children. Not like some people. And when they were bigger we all just worked as a team.

…But I'm very tired now, very tired…

My eyes close.

I die.

I just slip out of my body.

I'm looking down, and I can see them all. They're saying, "He's stopped breathing. He's gone."

Is your wife there as well?

Yes. She's crying and wailing and rocking and saying she doesn't want to live. It's a big ululating wail… but she's still got her daughters. I'm worried about her. There is no need for her to follow me so soon. My daughters are putting their arms around her and comforting her.[75] My Rebekkah was a good wife. She'll be alright, though, she's got all our sons and daughters—she could just live between all their households, or choose one to stay with—so she's not got any worries at all. She'll be fed and sheltered, and she's got all the grandchildren. She can watch them grow. I've no worries for the family I'm leaving behind. I did look after them. I did protect them, I did my best. And when my sons disobeyed me and went off with the soldiers and didn't hide, well, it still turned out alright, except for the youngest. And he could have died anyway, even if he'd stayed at home. There are plenty of accidents in life.

So you died, but there was no obvious contact with Jesus, was there?

Hmmm... ask me questions... it might come up then, because there's no obvious way at the moment.

So, what did you learn in that life?

To look after my family, to be kind to my children. You have to be firm but kind, and you have to let them go their own way a bit. There was no point being cross with them for going off with the soldiers, and it did turn out well, over all.

What did you learn that can help you now?

A sense of my own power and strength. I was formidable, well muscled, and intelligent enough to see bigger than the village, to see the problems, which is why I was looking at the battle. I just need to remember that, like then, I have the skills I need to complete my mission and bring my life to a successful close. So this is a good life to remember.

And I learned that you can die happy, and that you can die content. In this case it was just feeding the family and looking after them. But in my present life it's taking Jesus's words out to feed the world's spiritual hunger, and I'll do this by selling books and promoting them. But I do have enough strength and enough skill to do it, like I did in the other life, so that's a parallel with now. And if I look to see what's happening in the distance, I'll spot the troubles and the battles far off, and avoid them, like when we went up into the cave.

---

75 It's part of our culture to make a big noise like that. It's expected, and we were happy, we were close. Some wives are mightily glad when their husband dies.

Like you said, you don't have to get involved in other people's conflicts.

No, and they are quite happy to pull you in, and there's nothing in it for you, but it means you can't do what **your** actual job was. Die for some foreign king? And then your family dies because there's nobody there to feed them? That's ridiculous.

Let's look at who was who.

Ye then runs through the people who were in the life to see if any feel like people in my life now. Some do. Ye feels like Rebekkah.

Ye asks about the armies, about who was fighting.

Medes and Persians. I wasn't interested, they could keep their fights.[76]

The goats?

I loved those goats, they are almost like your children, your goats—and you see their offspring, like your children's children. They have pretty faces, lovely ears. They are fine creatures… and then you can eat them when they don't give you milk. Fine creatures… but I got more in the end. That was the worst thing, losing my goats. I knew there was a chance the boys would come back, but I knew the goats weren't ever coming back.

But the biggest surprise was the trader. When Ye asks about the trader, realization dawns.

---

76   King Cyrus came to the throne of Persia about 559 BC, when Persia was under the rule of the Medes. The Medes' kingdom lay just to the north of Persia, but it didn't take Cyrus long to conquer the Medes, and then together the Medes and Persians conquered the surrounding lands and established an empire.

So there was a lot of fighting in the area, and I feel my life was around then, in the middle of the first millenium BC, when Persia was an aggressive military power.

It was Cyrus who conquered Babylon and delivered the Jews from captivity, and there are many references to him in the Bible. Like the Jews, he believed in one God, and although he was a Zoroastrian he rebuilt their temple in Jerusalem at his own expense. When he died (either in 529 or 530 BC), he was succeeded by his son Cambyses, who died in 522 BC. Cambyses's son Darius the Great ruled until 486 BC, and he was succeeded by his son Xerxes, who ruled from 486 until his assassination in 465 BC. The Persian Empire just got bigger and bigger.

Persia is now Iran, and the Medes are the Kurds.

The trader was Jesus—but in an earlier incarnation, when he was getting the hang of Earth. He wasn't preaching a message but getting the hang of how it is to be here, because he'd been on different worlds. He was having to do a bit of homework for the coming "Savior" incarnation on Earth, because it is a very difficult world, this one.

He brought news which was helpful—hide your sons—trying to help us. (He brought news which was helpful when he came as Jesus, the Good News.) He learned about traveling because he was a trader, going on foot from community to community, which is what he had to do when he was doing his mission, his ministry. Learning to get on with different groups of people, to establish a rapport, or he would have gone hungry, wouldn't he? If you don't charm your way into a settlement... he was doing some homework there. I honored him as a guest, it was part of our culture anyway, and he liked my family. We fed him as well as we possibly could. We roasted a young male goat...

When Nadia heard him, deep down he wasn't a stranger, and she knew he brought good advice. She really listened and took notice. She came alive at that point, life became different, everything was seen very differently, and life had a very different purpose and focus for her after that.

The other message is **you never know whether the prophet is with you, you never know whether there are angels at your table. You never know who that stranger is,** and it touches you with humility, and you need to open your heart and give of your best, because you don't know. We could have turned him away with harsh words and said we hadn't got enough food to feed ourselves, but we didn't, we roasted a goat.

That's wild! I couldn't see any connections before.

It could be the Savior at your table when there's a knock at the door.

It's good to be kind and generous, because other people often have more to bestow than you, so if you're kind and generous who knows what might come back to you? Because you started the flow, in life, in the universe, and the flow always gets bigger. So what you set in motion comes back to you and gets better.

How does that life relate to you now?

About husbanding my resources... I'll always have enough, but not enough to squander. You don't eat your seed corn. (The Neal's Yard Remedies shop where I'd enjoyed working five hours a week ever since we'd been in the North East had just closed, a few days before.) Losing that job was like having my herd taken. The herd meant milk and cheese, even when you didn't eat the goats; it was sustenance. I'd loved the customers, the other girls in the shop, the herbal remedies, the lovely organic skin care products, and the company's environmental ethics. I'd loved helping people, and losing it had given me a feeling of loss.)

The treasure?

It was like an insurance policy for my family, they dug it up if they needed something. The insurance policy for my family now is their careers, their degrees are their treasure. They will always be able to earn money.

The son who died?

There's always that element in life. He was never as strong as the others, a bit foolish and easily led—but I don't think I got told the whole story. I suspect he got into an argument with one of the other soldiers... that there was some disgrace, but you don't have to know everything, especially if it would upset you.

It was time to consider if any healing was needed.

Ye asks if I need to release any emotions.

Yes—there was black in my throat when we started the life. Why was it there? Mmm... Because there were things I wanted to say that I didn't. I wanted to tell them off for wanting to go with the soldiers. I was **angry** and cross, but there was no point saying it. There was **agony**— the agony of the loss, and **disbelief** that it could have happened. I wanted to shout and rail at my wife and daughters, but there was no point because they couldn't have done anything. So I had to just not say it. **Loss, sadness, and grief**—for the sons and the goats. But I got more goats and the sons nearly all came back, and without the treasure my girls would not have made such good marriages, it was sons of the head of the village they'd married... so it's swings and roundabouts. **There were a lot of unsaid bitter words**, unsaid because I had enough self-control to know they would have been very harmful, but they poisoned me in a way. It was a **poison of the spirit, the black** (a higher level of poison than a physical one).

Ye asks me what color all this energy is.

Black and a slimy, dark blue—all in my throat.

Ye uses rattles and vocal sounds to help me break up the old stuck energy, and I release it to the angels, before healing and rebalancing my throat with pink and gold.

I know this will help me talk about the book better.

Ye asks if there is an affirmation I need, to create a new belief.

I consider… and say, "I am a tremendous success."

The color for this is turquoise, and I visualize the turquoise energy flowing into my throat.

Ye is now running through the standard list of things to do. He asks if there is a power animal I need to be connected to. Perhaps linked to my success?

I see a big eagle and a bison.

The eagle's gift is looking for trouble ahead and avoiding it in the bigger picture.

The bison's gift is to do with America. They were a mighty force in the old days, roaming in huge herds… and it calls to mind a shaman life when I wore a bison's horns and fur headdress…

Ye uses sound to strengthen the links to both my power animals.

There are no wounds to heal as I simply died of old age.

Any forgiveness needed?

I need to forgive the king for taking my sons.

The angels bring him. He's a man of learning and philosophy, but I tell him off, I get it all off my chest. He acknowledges the debt. Says he did his best with the plunder, and that they enjoyed it. But what about the one who died? I have to ask him that. The king says he'd have died anyway… I tell him I forgive him, and we hug.

The angels take the king away.

Was there any soul or spirit loss in that life?

Mmm...Yes. Spirit when my boys went, soul when my goats went.

I loved their silky ears, their fur, their big eyes. They're dumb but you can talk to them and tell them everything. You can stroke them, and they give you comfort. They like you, even though you're going to eat them... eventually... and they don't hold that against you. No, in a strange sort of way, they don't—"Better you than a lion, because there's no pain. It's quick and easy and you appreciate us and say thank you, and you actually look after us." ...I'm being shown it from the goats' point of view. Bless them.

Ye uses sound to help me, and I pull the soul and spirit fragments back through space and time, until they are above my physical body. They are cleansed. The spirit is to flow in through my thymus, into the upper chest, and the soul needs to go into my brow chakra, my third eye. There are sounds for all this.[77]

Is there any absolution needed to be given?

No, none needed.

Do you want to do a new future?

No, I did all I could. It was my sons' choices.

Is there anything you need to do in ordinary reality to follow up this work today?

Be more forceful, less tenuous, more black and white. Never mind fifty shades of gray, which side of the watershed does it fall on? Toward the black or toward the white? Decide, then that's all that matters.

The session enters the closing stages; I reinforce my link with the angels who look after my aura.

For me this is four angels of peace and my guardian angel. It's because when you're peaceful your aura is sound, when you get upset it perforates. The angels of peace are only small, more like cherubs, and the color of the link with them is rainbow colors. They are there to

---

77 "Trust" is the quality that returns with the spirit energy; I'd trusted my sons to obey me and respect my judgment. "Communication" is the quality that returns with the soul energy; it was never as easy to share the feelings of my heart after that—I'd talked to my goats a lot about how I felt about things. The replacement goats helped, but they were not as clever as mine. I'd mourned my goats every day for the rest of that life.

mend the holes if it's torn, they are troubleshooters.

I'm asked what color would really strengthen my aura today.

Pink and gold.

Ye uses tiny silver bells as I visualize pink and gold divine energy flowing in and suffusing my aura. When complete, I float up my body, through my crown, through the open cave bed, and back to the spirit of the cave—today it's the wolf, Silver Brother.

I have with me all the knowledge and understanding from that life long ago, and all the healing energies, the angelic links and the bison's and eagle's gifts.

Ye tells me to visualize Silver Brother closing the cave bed, and to thank him for helping today.

I do, but I have to laugh when the wolf replies, "Anytime, boss, just give the word." I'm having my face licked, big paws on my shoulder, and he's saying, "Never mind those goats, you've got me!"

...But Silver Brother is not alone. Jesus is with him.

Jesus is laughing. And I get told that though there might not have been much in the session today—compared to Nadia's and Mary's sessions—I needed to do it to make the most of his message. It will help me to deliver it better. I'm told that it's not always glamorous "bells and whistles" that come up in past lives, not always big important things, but that the plodding, mundane lives are the bricks in the wall that build it strong.[78] He says I did need to look at it today, it wasn't a luxury, but I don't need to do anymore past life sessions for *this* book. I've got his message, and that's what's important. Any more will confuse people. He says the Venus life, with its talk of the Divine Queen, addresses the Divine archetype imbalance—so that's good—but he says don't be surprised if you're asked to take it out! (Because it might be deemed too strange a chapter!)

And then it is time to go.

I climb the steps up the cave and come into present time.

78 Most past lives *are* humdrum, but it's surprising how much they resonate with your present life. There is a lot of treasure to be found in the humdrum. The basic currency of life never changes—family, love, relationships, food, and shelter. We have changed very little over the millennia, though the trappings of our lives may have.

And I smell the lovely fragrance of Aura-Soma's Serapis Bey quintessence on Ye's hands, which are now gently cradling my head. (We use drops of the fragrant liquid at the beginning too, and the scent association helps me to know I'm back.)

We thank the Archangels Michael, Uriel, Gabriel, and Raphael for their help. And then, after a gentle scalp rub which grounds me, I roll over on to my left side and curl up like a baby in the womb. Ye puts the blanket right over me, head and body, so that I'm in a womb-like space. This is to symbolize being born into my new understanding, my new karmic pattern.

And while Ye goes to put the kettle on, I slowly pull back the blanket. It's like having had a transfusion of light. Pink and gold light.

***

I felt really good after the session. You are always filled with wonder, and further ramifications of the story may fall into place in the days that follow. Who knew goats are such fabulous creatures?!

It is beautiful work, and as you've seen in this example, even a straightforward died-of-old-age life can benefit from healing, and many lives need more than this, as the next chapter will show. It is worth remembering that you can release the cause of *why* things have gone wrong just as easily as releasing emotions. And heavy karma such as curses, black magic influences, or poison residues—think Nazi gas chambers—are no problem either, no more difficult than releasing emotions.

One of my demonstration volunteers once wanted to look at why she was having difficulty with money. She went back to a life in World War 2 when she was a rich Jewish woman living in Germany. She had a lovely home and a family, but the house was confiscated and she was shipped off to a concentration camp. She spent her last days in rags and died in a gas chamber. After she had reviewed the life she could see that having money made her feel vulnerable, so subconsciously she would sabotage her financial situation because her subconscious wanted to keep her safe. It was a way of protecting her, but obviously not very helpful today!

We did the appropriate healing and released the residual energy of the gas she was still carrying, but then I asked her to look at *why* this had happened to her, and she found it was because of an abuse of sex magic in ancient Egypt. There was a symbol to encapsulate this energy, and she released it with the help of the rattles and the archangels. We didn't need to go into the Egyptian story, direct knowing came with the symbol, and that was enough.

So no matter what, we do not need to be a slave to our past.

If you have the courage to look, you can set yourself free. That is the wonder of past lives. But when it comes to difficult past lives there are few that could beat the one in the next chapter. It affected me badly for three hundred years. But from it I gleaned a warning about our future...

Chapter 15
The Sphinx and the Hall of Records

AHMET'S Story

The Great Sphinx of Egypt is sitting on a secret. The secret has a direct bearing on our immediate future.

The Sphinx is old, even older than many people think. It is carved from a rocky outcrop on the Giza plateau, which lies outside the ancient city of Cairo. It has always been draped in mystery, the Sphinx. And no wonder when you know its story.

I was there when it was carved, so I should know... but then I was a young lad called Ahmet. As an apprentice painter I worked in the Hall of Records that was cut from the stone beneath it. The Hall is the reason for the Sphinx: the stone lion was to be a guardian and marker to prevent the Hall being lost in the sands of time. And indeed the Sphinx has been buried by drifting desert sand several times over the past millennia—last being dug out in 1905 to reveal paws fifty feet long.

I saw its secrets thousands of years ago and paid for this knowledge with my life.

I share it with you now.

For this is the apocalypse, the time of revealing.[79]

Let the secrets of the ages be uncovered.

For we have nothing to fear.

---

79 Literally that is what "apocalypse" means—it just means un-covering, a lifting of the veil or revelation, the disclosure of something hidden. It does not mean a catastrophic event. It is a disaster only for those who've been getting away with things that shock us when they come to light.

But those who have sought to manipulate us … oh, they do.

***

In ancient Egypt in the far-off days of the Age of Leo (circa 10,500–8000 BC), I was born to a poor family who scraped a living in the shanty town huddled outside the walls of the grand king's palace. My father was not given to hard work, my mother was shrill and sharp with her tongue, and food was scarce. I had younger sisters but no brothers.

As soon as I was old enough I began to search for employment. Wandering the lanes of the souk I found a perfume seller looking for an apprentice. He agreed to take me on. My mother pursed her lips and thought the money not enough. I longed to work with oils and beautiful scents, to sell them to the fine ladies I saw calling… but before anything could come of my young boy's dreams an extraordinary thing happened that turned our world upside down.

Among the stars of night there shone one of surpassing beauty. It grew larger than all others until it rivaled the sun, and we thought it was a star falling to Earth and we clustered on the banks of the great Nile River to watch as it came down.

People thronged to see such a sign of wonder.

Priests left their temples, the palace emptied, and we watched, all of us, mouths and eyes open in wonder as the star landed on the far bank, across the shimmering, shining water from us.

The night sky was filled with thunder and lightning.

Water and frogs scooped up from the Nile crashed down around us in a terrifying deluge. Fear was struck in our hearts by terrible sounds and a communication of sorts began. In our minds we heard it. In stern and mighty fashion, words boomed inside our heads:

Listen slaves!

Prostrate yourselves in the face of the mighty!

We have journeyed far!

We bring you that which you must know!

We are Gods!

You dare to wreck our handiwork!

By which they meant the proper ordering of the worlds. But what had we done?

...No—it wasn't that—it was what we were *going* to do...

And so they called for the priests to approach, bowed low in penitence and awe, and then communication began in earnest.

We were told we were one of the chosen peoples.[80] We were to receive and record information to prevent a very bad thing from happening—a disaster so big it would affect even the home of the gods. And so it was that the instructions to prepare the chamber that would become the Hall of Records, as well as the information it contains, came directly from the squid-and-octopus-like, water-dwelling beings from Sirius that we were beginning to see in our mind's eye.

It was a night like no other and it changed everything.

Over the next two years the resources of our king and of our temples were channeled to their will. There was no shortage of well-paid work when the Sphinx was being carved from the stone of the plateau and master craftsmen toiled night and day to obey their instructions. My mother gave me no peace unless I worked ceaselessly. We had to complete the vision the priests had been given or risk being annihilated by the anger of these gods. And as time passed an understanding of their story and of their need arose. We never saw them directly, but the power of their minds was enough. Their purpose was clear, the instructions exact.

If the bad thing happened because we on Earth got it wrong, the shock waves would travel down the energy grids of the universe and affect the worlds around Star-Sirius—affect the worlds the gods loved, and loved so much that they had taken the trouble to travel back in time to try to prevent the catastrophic disaster that was the "bad thing."

---

80 Others consider themselves "the chosen people of God" too, and this may give a clue as to who else was entrusted with the message. (Don't be put off by the difference between God and Gods, because in Genesis, the oldest part of the Bible, there is no problem with the plural. Chapter 1, verse 26, says, "And God said, Let **us** make man in **our** image ...")

I rather suspect Jerusalem's very ancient reputation as a holy city stems from this time, and that something was hidden there.

The knowledge was left in at least three different places in the world.

But they had been here before.[81]

They had visited Earth long before people walked the planet, and they had introduced life-forms into our seas; cephalopods like squids and octopuses are in their debt. When the bad thing happened, like detectives, they had traced backward down the time line we had woven. And it was major events in this time line that we were to record and paint—thousands of years of things yet to happen, from where we were standing.

They had come looking for societies that were organized well enough to work for them. They found several, and left the information in various locations, but we Egyptians were particularly well suited to their needs and had the means to create the most splendid record.

Over the time it took our stonemasons to carve out the chamber for the Hall of Records beneath the Sphinx, the master painters made daily trips to the Star That Landed. On clay tablets and papyrus they faithfully recorded the images they were shown in their minds. They returned with the tablets and painted the information on long pieces of woven cloth, thus creating the portable record. This was rolled up and carried into the Hall when the chamber was ready to receive the permanent record on its walls.

At the time of construction there were two ways in. A wide entrance was cut into the stone of the plateau to allow workers like us access, but on completion it would be blocked and carefully concealed—because a second route was planned to allow for the chamber being discovered. This narrow, twisting, and booby-trapped passageway ensured the discoverer would have to jump down into the chamber from a height. The weight of a human body hitting the floor was important. The vibrations would set something off.

The floor was circular and the chamber arching over it a hemisphere. The "something" was in a second chamber below, and this, with the chamber above, completed a sphere. It's possible that a granite pyramidal cap protected the Hall of Records from rainwater percolating down, but it was definitely pale honey-colored limestone that we painted on.

By the time we had finished our work the curved walls and domed ceiling were entirely covered with pictures and hieroglyphs embellished

---

81 They had history here because their home directly resonates with the energies of our world, and in some way their world is a twin of Earth and on the same energy line in the universe.

in gold. It would not have been stretching the truth to describe the chamber as "the circle of gold" because the pictures were arranged in bands circling and spiraling round the walls depicting three alternative time lines.

The time lines were like a plait made of three strands, and they hold information on three possible futures; key events throughout the millennia are recognizably painted there. We called the upper strand the "blue" band, and it shows the events of our optimum achievable future, a heaven on Earth for humankind. The middle strand was the "white" band, showing the events of a stable achievable future, while the lowest strand was the "red" band and concerned a future more like hell on Earth. All the wars we have fought were painted in the red band.

The work took two long years to complete. And as I worked I was curious about what the other masters were painting in the strands of time. My master had been assigned to start his painting at the epoch change that brought in the Age of Pisces, [82] heralding the birth of Jesus the Christ, and so we began our work there, but I liked to see the other ages when I got the chance. In my short breaks I often scrambled up the ladders and scaffolding to look.

I was very taken with the doings of Atlantis throughout the ages of Cancer, Gemini, and Taurus—but what I liked best were the pictures of the catastrophe that destroyed it! Atlantis was such an unassailable ruling power when I was the young lad Ahmet that this was difficult to imagine, and the pictures were as exciting to me then as a disaster movie would be today.

---

82 Zodiacal Ages: The zodiac is a star map that helped the ancients to navigate time. It allowed them to divide time into Ages, each approximately 2,160 years long—because that's how long it took for the constellation on the dawn horizon at the time of the spring equinox to change. The constellation lent its name to the Age. The tilt in the Earth's axis causes this change, and it means every 26,000 years the Earth wheels slowly backward through the twelve signs of the zodiac. This makes a Great Year, each age being a Great Month. At the moment we are leaving the Age of Pisces behind and entering the Age of Aquarius as we step into a new Great Year. A whole new cycle of time lies before us.

I'd just like to mention that although we called them "blue," "white," and "red," the bands may not literally have been painted solidly in those colors—which is why at first I used quotation marks when referring to them.

Over time we have soared into the blue and sunk into the red, but overall we have stabilized out in the white. Well, that's how it was until the end of the Age of Pisces brought World Wars 1 and 2, and from that point on we slipped further and further into red, with the result that the United States is now in red and is pulling Africa and Britain in too. Australia and some other countries are still in white, and small countries and tiny islands that have not been so much affected by our civilization are in blue, with Tibet playing a major role in holding the balance. The Tibetans are a very strong people who have kept their personal consciousness in the blue heaven state despite terrible troubles with China. But of all the things Ahmet saw the most significant for us now was this: as we cross into the Age of Aquarius the red band terminates abruptly and with great finality. It happens in one of two ways:

a) either we get it very right and abandon wars, or

b) we get it terribly wrong and no longer exist to wage them.

***

And the Sirians will know when we find the chamber. Sensors in a robotic device beneath the floor detect life-forms entering and emit a signal home. The device is the "something" I referred to earlier.[83]

Our extraterrestrial visitors left other things behind too. They left a discreet calling card in the Hall, to make sure there would be no mistaking the provenance of the knowledge there: in the center of the floor is a small metallic sphere. It is a model of Earth *as seen from space,* dense and very heavy, thinly covered in gold and displayed within a triangle of extraterrestrial metal.

Three rods of "star metal" form the triangle.

It is an isosceles triangle, with two long sides of equal length and a short third side. The shape has a special significance. It was chosen to symbolize the end of conflict and the emergence of a new way of

83 A section of the floor lifts up and gives access to the lower chamber housing the device, and there is also a concealed passage hidden in the walls linking the two chambers. Ahmet thought the priests had really overstepped the mark and killed a god when he saw the device lying in its own sarcophagus in the Chamber of the Guardians. (In the regression session I felt that it should have been placed upright, not lying down, and wondered if it would still work. But I expect the Sirians would have intervened if not, because they checked the progress of the work frequently by reading the minds of those who had seen it, when they came to give their daily report.

being. Two sides make for conflict, but the emerging third side heralds resolution and the new angle we need to develop in the way we see things.[84]

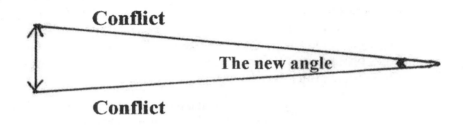

The sphere rests on a floor that is patterned with curves radiating out from the center. The patterns concern star alignments and the energy lines that Earth is on in the universe. These universal "ley lines" are fixed points, and as the Earth moves in orbit she travels along and across them following the wanderings of our sun. Cream, brown, red, and white tiles were used to lay out what is an unnaturally flat floor.

And never underestimate Egyptian magic.

My paralyzed but still living body was entombed beneath the chamber because the priests decided we were to be *the guardians through time*. We had no idea what was coming until it was too late to escape, and we were forced to take the secrets of the Sphinx with us to the grave.

This is why I'm sharing them with the world. I owe it to Ahmet—and it is time.

My bones are still there, and I believe the pattern of my incarnations was interrupted because of all the soul and spirit energy that was deliberately trapped. Intervention by higher beings such as angels can pull you out of the back of the painted spells, but it is like being caught and held in a magnetic field of one-dimensional reality. It has you frozen, suspended in time, unable to think and devoid of the awareness to fight back. Not nice at all.

It happened like this.

---

84 The shape has a link with the many sightings of triangular UFOs since the 1990s. Subliminally they prod our collective consciousness into remembering.

When the work was completed there was a great feast of celebration at the palace. And as you know, my family was poor. I was excited to be invited. I had never been in the palace, never mind at a banquet with the king, and this day started out as the best day of my life. But in the evening after the feasting and the food, when we were content and happy and the sharpness of our minds had gone, then it was we were given one last drink of drugged wine, "a special draught for the workers," it was said. The paralyzing poison took hold, and we fell off the benches one by one. We lay helpless on the floor unable to move. Others thought us drunk, but this was a cruel deceit.

And one by one we were gathered up, placed on stretchers, and carried off to the priests. In the secrecy of priestly confines our bodies were prepared and sponged down with sweet-smelling herbs and ointments.

Priests slit my body and placed a crystal within my solar plexus. They stitched the cut together, not to help me, but to keep the crystal surely in its place. Then they tied a magical talisman about my neck, which tied me to their service and laid claim to me, and claim even to my spirit bodies.

We were all treated thus, and when we were readied ritual garments were put on us. With my feet wrapped diagonally in strips of cloth (and done so with care so turquoise bands alternated with gold), I was cut off from the energies of the Earth below. Then was I cut off from the energy of the gods above, and with great care the magic was woven that would bind my ka (spirit body essence) in limbo, serving their purpose as their slave.

Paralyzed and prepared, we were laid out in open sarcophagi. In procession were we taken down to the Sphinx, but this time we did not enter the Hall of our toil. No, we were carried beneath and no longer was the cavernous emptiness of the second chamber a puzzlement; the purpose was clear.

In soft lamplight we were placed in our position for eternity, unable to move muscle or utter sound. We could not speak to curse, though anger near choked me with burning words unsaid.

And as our golden paintings sparkled on the walls above we waited, helpless, as the priests continued with their work. Arrayed in their magnificence they chanted and weaved about our stilled bodies, intent to the last on stealing our souls and spirits with their magic.

Then they were done.

Out they filed.

Leaving us alone and bound to our fate.

As footsteps faded the air grew silent save for the sound of blocks of stone being guided into place.

Soon the entrance which had been so familiar was no more. Lamps guttered. And when the darkness came, with it came difficulty in breathing. Finally breathing ceased. But I did not rise up out of my body and pass into the light of the spiritual worlds. I was held fast by the force of the magic. It would be quite some time before I rejoined the flow of life in the universe.

***

At the end of the session, in the expanded awareness that comes with death, I realized that neither the king nor the Sirians had required this sacrifice from us. It was the priests' idea, and afterward they had bought the silence of our families.

And as you can imagine, when it came to the healing repair work there was a lot more to do than usual. Most past life sessions take two hours. This took five on a cold February afternoon in 1997, exactly a year before the Hall of Records was due to be found. I can only hope that one day soon we will be hearing something of its discovery.[85]

---

85 I presented this material in a talk for the Mind Body Spirit Northern Festival at G-Mex in Manchester later that year, because I wanted the world to know. I wanted to bear witness and to honor what Ahmet had brought us. I was also invited down to Cornwall to speak at a UFO conference, and I included it in the material presented there.

I hoped we'd be hearing about the chamber in the news in 1998—but of course that didn't happen, and officially, we're all still waiting. Determined efforts by various people did make the news, including someone who went out to Egypt claiming to have the sound keys to open the chamber. I found out that Edgar Cayce had predicted it would be opened in 1998. But we're all still waiting because the powers-that-be have obstructed it, for reasons best known to themselves.

One of my most talented past life students did the session for me while I lived in Manchester, and with the archangels' assistance she helped me release whatever was left of the other poor souls that had been trapped there with me. We released the many energy traces of the priests' magical handiwork that were still in my subtle bodies; and reclaimed my soul and spirit fragments from beneath the Sphinx—and we did a new future, exploring an alternative time line where I was

After writing this chapter I was curious about the Egyptian hieroglyph for Sirius, and I could hardly believe my eyes when I saw it. It comprised three symbols: a star, a hemisphere, and a triangle. Looking at it now I could read Sirius as "The Star, bringer of the Chamber & Triangle (of star metal)." Perhaps the symbols are just an amazing coincidence, but what are the chances of that? After all, it would have been the priests who created the hieroglyphs, as they safeguarded all knowledge.

Hieroglyph for Sirius

The Sphinx is generally mistakenly attributed to the pharaoh Kafra, simply because he vandalized it. Around 2500 BC he had the lion's head carved down into a representation of his own. However, when you look at it today the pharaoh's head looks too small for the lion's body and fails to match the heavy erosion clearly visible on the limestone of the body; geology provides evidence for the true age of the Sphinx.

Egypt's climate today is hot and dry but in the Age of Leo (circa 10,500–8000 BC) the area was much wetter. The Sphinx shows damage by wind and sand as you would expect, but the ancient limestone of its body also bears the scars of extensive rainfall erosion. For this to have happened, it must have been exposed to the rains marking the transition of northern Africa from the last Ice Age to the present interglacial epoch. This transition occurred through the Ages of Leo and Cancer, in the millennia from 10,000 to 5000 BC.

apprenticed to the perfumer as I'd originally wanted, working with fine oils and scents instead of preparing paints for the better paid work my mother insisted on at the Sphinx. But I can tell you, this is not a life I'd have wanted to access with any other system of regression. This was heavy. I needed the therapist's powerful shamanic rattles to help me release the energies from the past.

At the spring equinox when it was first carved in the Age of Leo, the lion-headed Sphinx would have gazed directly at the lion Leo in the stars.

There was time-coded protection around the booby-trapped entrance that was set to decay by 1998, enabling the chamber to be found in safety and its secrets revealed to the world. The information held there was designed for us, in our time, and it is an extreme catalyst for change. That is its sole purpose. It is to shock us into action by showing graphically where we've been and where we are heading if we do not change direction. And because it is full of information that should not have been available back then, the truth of the future predictions will be indisputable. The perpetrators of many false flag events that have warped the history of the last decades will have their cover blown. They are revealed on the walls of the chamber. It will be their apocalypse—disgraced, exposed, and no longer able to manipulate us. And so although the information can not be misused there is always the very real possibility that it can be suppressed, which may well be why the world is still waiting.

Since the Sphinx was built, Cairo has expanded greatly. It has sprawled out toward the plateau and affected the water table in the area. This has risen and although several passages have been found round the Sphinx during restoration work, at both the rear and the paws, they appear to be flooded. For this reason, officially, it is said that they have not been explored—but I can't help thinking one leads down to the Hall of Records and somebody knows what's there!

***

The message from the records is that *the time of choice is upon us*, and what will save the world, if we are to be saved, is **the goodness in the hearts of ordinary people, and their common sense**. The change needed will not come from the top down but from the grass roots up.

We wake up to our power whenever we say, "That's enough" or, "Not in my name." All signs of protest, whistle blowing, uncovering of corruption, people living through their consciences and coming together—whether to save a tree, ban blood sports or cruel farming practices, protest at the greed of bankers—all these things are pointers to the way forward and give hope that we are waking from the sleep of the ages and coming into our power in time to make a difference.

What we do in our own lives matters.

It's as though the Egyptian god Anubis has all our hearts in his scales. Will they be as light as the feather he balances each heart against? Light because they are filled with love and joy? Light enough to take us on to eternal life and assure our species' continued tenure of this planet? Or will they weigh so heavy with greed, hate, and bitter, reckless selfishness that we will be tipped straight back into the Creator's recycling bin for failed species when the choice point comes?

In the chamber the white and blue bands did continue on, proving it is possible to fulfill Jesus's prophecy when he said:

Blessed are the meek, for they shall inherit the Earth.

It's only the meek who can. The war boys of the military industrial complex are running out of time and swimming against a cosmic tide. They will be swept away; but it falls to us to choose how—and whether or not we are taken with them.

We wounded our time line with Jesus's crucifixion, and the message from the Hall of Records is that we teeter on the brink of a final cataclysmic wound from which our time line—at present the red one— won't recover. We need to rise up and find our way into the white, and even better, the blue. That's why what we do in our own lives matters.

How we think and act can make a huge difference.

We already have everything we need to make Aquarius a Golden Age. Jesus was with us such a short time, but he brought us all the tools we need to heal our hearts and nourish our souls and spirits. He gave us the compass to find our way to the golden lands of the future, both in this world and the next. **We wrote Jesus's words down in the Bible, but now it's time to write them in our hearts.**

The Great Sphinx: The photographs were taken in October 2001. In the lower one you see the largest of the pyramids and evidence of lots of activity going on around the Sphinx. Tourists were not allowed near this area. We had to photograph from a designated place, and you can just see the edge of the high ground we were standing on if you look carefully at the upper photograph. You can see the huge paws and the lack of erosion on the small head contrasting well with the badly eroded body.

Acknowledgments

Ye Min for your love and support through the long years of my writing, Veronica Fyland for your friendship and skill with regression, Isabelle Crummie for your enthusiasm, inspiration, and questions! Hana Kanoo for your friendship and for the laptop that made it all possible, Guy Steven Needler for your excellent advice and help, Sam and Jean Wright for your support and for the many Probe International conferences, which is how I met Guy! Dolores Cannon for blazing the trail, Julia Cannon for taking things forward, Nancy Vernon for your wisdom and kindness, my editor Debbie Upton for being an absolute joy to work with, Brandy and the lovely people at Ozark Mountain Publishing – you have all helped me much more than you will ever know. To you, and to my guides and the angels,

THANK YOU!

Working with Time

In our lifetimes we enrich and develop our souls through the interplay of spirit with matter, and at the end of each life we return to our home in the spiritual worlds. We leave the levels of illusion and come to rest in the heart and mind of the Creator where all things have their being: all that has been, all that is, all that will be is contained within that consciousness.

Time is not purely the linear construct we experience in our lives, because there is more to time than a simple one-way flow. A DVD does not cease to exist after you have viewed its contents, and the past does not cease to exist because your consciousness has experienced it. The DVD has a beginning, middle, and end, and so do our lives. We have multichoice options so which end we see depends on our choices, but all possibilities already exist within the mind of the Creator.

Time travel is theoretically possible, *but we can simply transcend time by altering our level of consciousness*. This is how remote viewing is possible and how past life therapy works. The past is another country but we can visit. It still lives within our psyche, as do our possible futures. Because it still lives, healing the past is powerful and the ripples of change reach the future. This makes me effective when I work as a past life therapist, and it is how I came by the information in this book.

It is always of great benefit to remember that you have lived before, and will again; to realize that you are indestructible, eternal spirit adventuring through time; and to see the ease with which you transition through death. This can remove a lot of fear. But even if you never seek out a therapist to help you find your inner treasures, you can always be your own past life detective and deduce some of your lives for yourself.

By considering the time periods that interest you, you can work out *when* you've lived, and from which countries you long to visit you can work out *where* you've lived before. Perhaps you love Indian or Chinese food? Do you pick Mediterranean plants for your garden? What films or books have really come alive for you?—consider when they were set.

It's amazing how close the memories are, and sometimes they surface in dreams... but what attracts us is where we've been happy, and what repels us is where we haven't, because our subconscious is trying to protect us from a repeat. But one thing you can bank on is that **you have a lot of hidden treasures!**

Recommended Reading

Denise Linn's *Past Lives, Present Miracles* gives you simple ways to access and work with your own past lives at home. Well worth a read.

The Inner Guide Meditation by Edwin C. Steinbrecher is excellent if you want a simple way to meet up with your own guides, and learn from them. I never got as far as the tarot and astrology work, but meeting a guide was so easy. This is how I met Francis.

The Wisdom of Near Death Experiences: How Understanding NDEs Can Help Us Live More Fully by Dr. Penny Satori. An excellent book. Of course, few of us have NDEs, but almost anyone can look at one of their own past lives and take comfort in that.

Soul Speak: The Language of Your Body by Julia Cannon. As Julia says, we are masters of manifestation. Discover what YOU are trying to say to YOURSELF.

Heal Your Body by Louise Hay is excellent for understanding your body's messages, and it provides affirmations for healing. A very positive book about living, of benefit to everyone.

Further along this line of inquiry is *The Healing Power of Illness* by Thorwald Dethtefsen and Rutiger Dahlke, MD; it's a very interesting and eye-opening book.

There is also much esoteric knowledge in *Further Dimensions of Healing Addictions* by Donna Cunningham, MSW, and Andrew Ramer—and the addictions covered include such everyday substances as coffee, wine, beer, sugar, and tobacco. The book explains the whys, the karma, and the effect on the chakras, and most importantly what you can do about the addictions.

If I could give you one gift it would be to **think of yourself as lucky.** The most powerful affirmation I have personally found is "I am a lucky woman" or "I am so lucky"—just saying it gives rise to a feeling of gratitude, which attracts more luck—and even if things are going badly it makes me laugh, and I feel better. So either way I win! In *The Luck Factor*, Professor Richard Wiseman, a research psychologist, offers four simple principles that will change your luck—and your life.

Julie Lomas's *Comfy Slippers and a Cup of Tea* is an easy to read self-help book, full of wisdom. A little friend to dip into.

Al Koran's *Bring Out the Magic in Your Mind* was one of the very first life-changing books I ever read, and I still have a soft spot for it. It's a very good place to start.

And for help with positive thinking I suggest Norman Vincent Peale's *The Power of Positive Thinking*. This book has been around for a very long time, but it still works!

The books of Dolores Cannon contain a lot of knowledge. There are two about Jesus, *They Walked with Jesus* and *Jesus and the Essenes*. Others concern the volunteers who have incarnated to help Earth at this crucial time. Few consciously remember, but they find Earth life more difficult than they ever imagined—coming, as they do, from other dimensions and from other worlds. They have come to help us raise our collective consciousness, to help prevent the looming wound in our time line. But they often feel the odd one out in their family, or pine for an undefined place called "home"... and sadly many take a shortcut out of their embodiment to return home. It is undeniable that this is a time when there is an epidemic of sensitive young people taking their own lives, when perhaps, if only they'd realized they were here on a mission, it could have made all the difference. I read Dolores's *Keepers of the Garden* a very long time ago, and since then she has written *The Three Waves of Volunteers and the New Earth*, *The Convoluted Universe* series, and *The Search for Hidden Knowledge*. In her regression work Dolores has certainly come across some remarkable material and pushed the boundaries of our understanding.

Guy Steven Needler's books cover new ground when it comes to our understanding of God. He has written *The History of God, Beyond the Source: Book 1, Beyond the Source: Book 2, How to Avoid Karma*, and *The Origin Speaks*. And just like this book, his contain keys to raise our consciousness, although neither of us knows what the keys are!

The Mystery of the Crystal Skulls by Chris Morton and Ceri Louise Thomas is not only a good read but it's the book that sparked my writing. Fascinating and informative; read it, and you will understand why my next book is *Holy Ice*.

Holy Ice will be all about the secrets of the skulls that transcend time, accessed through my past lives, and stretching through the dimensions to other worlds. The skulls may be an enigma, but they are adept at surviving crises and the changes of world ages. They survived Atlantis, and I wanted to know what they could tell us about the looming wound in our time line. I wouldn't have missed this research for anything!

The secrets revealed in *Holy Ice* and later *Divine Fire* underline just how crucial Jesus's message is for us in the coming times. If those who forget the past are doomed to repeat its mistakes, then this truly is a time to remember. When we see where we've come from it's so much easier to see where we are heading, and so the stories in my next book piece together the map of time.

For in the past we will find the keys to the future.

Bibliography

Books referred to in the text:

Bek, Lilla, and Annie Wilson. *What Colour Are You?* London: Thorsons (HarperCollins), 1981.

Bible: *The Holy Bible*, rev. ed. Cambridge: Cambridge University Press, 1924.

Cannon, Dolores. *Keepers of the Garden.* Huntsville, AR: Ozark Mountain Publishing, 1993; rptd. 1995, 2002, 2008, 2009, 2010, 2011, 2012, 2013, 2014, 2015.

Castaneda, Carlos. *The Teachings of Don Juan.* Berkeley: University of California Press, 1968. Published in Penguin Books 1970; rptd. 1972, 1973, 1974, 1975, 1976, 1978, 1979, 1981, 1982.

Easton, M. G. *Illustrated Bible Dictionary*, 1st ed. London: T. Nelson and Sons, 1893.

Fyfe, Atasha. *Magic Past Lives.* London: Hay House, 2013.

The Findhorn Community. *The Findhorn Garden.* London: Turnstone Books and Wildwood House, 1976.

Ingerman, Sandra. *Soul Retrieval: Mending the Fragmented Self.* New York: HarperCollins, 1991.

Kindred Spirit. Magazine. London.

Lamborn Wilson, Peter. *Angels.* London: Thames and Hudson, 1980.

Linn, Denise. *Past Lives, Present Miracles: How to Use Reincarnation for Personal Growth.* (My copy bears the original title: *Past Lives, Present Dreams.* London: Judy Piatkus, 1994.)

Morton, Chris, and Ceri Louise Thomas. *The Mystery of the Crystal Skulls: Unlocking the Secrets of the Past, Present, and Future.* London: Thorsons, an imprint of Harper Collins, 1997.

Needler, Guy Steven. *The History of God.* Huntsville, AR: Ozark Mountain Publishing, 2011.

Needler, Guy Steven. *Beyond the Source: Book 1.* Huntsville, AR: Ozark Mountain Publishing, 2012.

Needler, Guy Steven. *Beyond the Source: Book 2.* Huntsville, AR: Ozark Mountain Publishing, 2013.

Needler, Guy Steven. *Avoiding Karma.* Huntsville, AR: Ozark Mountain Publishing, 2014.

Needler, Guy Steven. *The Origin Speaks.* Huntsville, AR: Ozark Mountain Publishing, 2015.

Rossetti, Francesca. *Psycho-Regression: A New System for Healing and Personal Growth.* London: Judy Piatkus, 1992.

Sams, Jamie, and David Carson. *The Medicine Cards.* Santa Fe, NM: Bear & Company, 1988.

Steinbrecher, Edwin C. *The Inner Guide Meditation: A Transformational Journey to Enlightenment and Awareness.* Wellingborough, Northamptonshire: Aquarian Press, 1982; rptd. 1983, 1985.

Steiner, Rudolph. *Manifestations of Karma.* London: Rudolph Steiner Press of London, 1976; rptd. 1996.

Taylor, Allegra. *I Fly Out with Bright Feathers: The Quest of a Novice Healer.* London: Fontana Paperbacks and simultaneously in hardback by William Collins, 1987.

Whitton, Joel L., and Joe Fisher. *Life between Life.* London: Grafton, an imprint of HarperCollins, 1987.

Yogananda, Paramahansa. *Autobiography of a Yogi.* Los Angeles: Self Realization Fellowship, 1979.

Young, Alan. *Spiritual Healing: Miracle or Mirage?* Marina del Rey, CA: DeVorss, 1981.

About the Author

Paulinne Delcour-Min is a regression therapist, artist and teacher. Over the years she has helped many people review and learn from their past lives in order to benefit their present one. Her passion for understanding her own previous life times has led to an extraordinary journey which she shares with us through her books.

After raising her family, she now lives by the sea in the North East of England with her husband, who is also a writer and therapist. She would love to hear from you and can be contacted through her website.

www.paulinnedelcour-min.com

If you liked this book, you might also like:

Between Death & Life
by Dolores Cannon

The Anne Dialogues
by Guy Needler

A Funny Thing Happen on the Way to Heaven
by Grant Pealer

The Dawn Book
by Annie Stillwater Gray

Live from the Other Side
by Maureen McGill & Nola Davis

Holiday in Heaven
by Aron Abrahamsen

For more information about any of the above titles, soon to be released titles,
or other items in our catalog, write, phone or visit our website:
Ozark Mountain Publishing, Inc.
PO Box 754, Huntsville, AR 72740
479-738-2348
www.ozarkmt.com

For more information about any of the titles published by Ozark Mountain Publishing, Inc., soon to be released titles, or other items in our catalog, write, phone or visit our website:

Ozark Mountain Publishing, Inc.

PO Box 754

Huntsville, AR 72740

479-738-2348/800-935-0045

www.ozarkmt.com

Other Books by Ozark Mountain Publishing, Inc.

Other Books by Ozark Mountain Publishing, Inc.

Sherry O'Brian
Peaks and Valleys
Riet Okken
The Liberating Power of Emotions
Victor Parachin
Sit a Bit
Nikki Pattillo
A Spiritual Evolution
Children of the Stars
Rev. Grant H. Pealer
A Funny Thing Happened on the
    Way to Heaven
Worlds Beyond Death
Victoria Pendragon
Born Healers
Feng Shui from the Inside, Out
Sleep Magic
The Sleeping Phoenix
Michael Perlin
Fantastic Adventures in Metaphysics
Walter Pullen
Evolution of the Spirit
Debra Rayburn
Let's Get Natural with Herbs
Charmian Redwood
A New Earth Rising
Coming Home to Lemuria
David Rivinus
Always Dreaming
M. Don Schorn
Elder Gods of Antiquity
Legacy of the Elder Gods
Gardens of the Elder Gods
Reincarnation...Stepping Stones of Life
Garnet Schulhauser
Dance of Eternal Rapture

Dance of Heavenly Bliss
Dancing Forever with Spirit
Dancing on a Stamp
Annie Stillwater Gray
Education of a Guardian Angel
The Dawn Book
Work of a Guardian Angel
Blair Styra
Don't Change the Channel
Natalie Sudman
Application of Impossible Things
L.R. Sumpter
The Old is New
We Are the Creators
Janie Wells
Embracing the Human Journey
Payment for Passage
Dennis Wheatley/ Maria Wheatley
The Essential Dowsing Guide
Maria Wheatley
Druidic Soul Star Astrology
Jacquelyn Wiersma
The Zodiac Recipe
Sherry Wilde
The Forgotten Promise
Lyn Willmoth
A Small Book of Comfort
Stuart Wilson & Joanna Prentis
Atlantis and the New Consciousness
Beyond Limitations
The Essenes -Children of the Light
The Magdalene Version
Power of the Magdalene
Robert Winterhalter
The Healing Christ

For more information about any of the above titles, soon to be released titles,
or other items in our catalog, write, phone or visit our website:
PO Box 754, Huntsville, AR 72740
479-738-2348/800-935-0045
www.ozarkmt.com